The World of
Manet

TIME
LIFE
BOOKS
®

TIME-LIFE LIBRARY OF ART

The World of
Manet

1832-1883

by Pierre Schneider
and
the Editors of TIME-LIFE BOOKS

TIME-LIFE BOOKS, New York

About the Author

Pierre Schneider, who also wrote *The World of Watteau* in this series, was born in Antwerp and educated in the United States, receiving his Ph.D. at Harvard University, where he was a member of the Society of Fellows. Art critic for the weekly journal *L'Express* in Paris since 1958, Mr. Schneider has also been a contributing editor for *Art News;* his articles are frequently found in *Horizon* and *The New York Times Magazine.* His books include a study of Nicolas Poussin, a collection of essays on poets and painters, and a revealing series of dialogues about the Louvre with contemporary artists. In 1967, Mr. Schneider was the organizer of an international symposium on the poet-critic Charles Baudelaire; during the following year he produced and wrote programs on art for French television. He lives in Paris with his wife and two daughters.

The Consulting Editor

H.W. Janson is Professor of Fine Arts at New York University, where he is also Chairman of the Department of Fine Arts at Washington Square College. Among his numerous publications are *History of Art* and *The Sculpture of Donatello.*

The Consultant for This Book

Theodore Reff, Professor of Art History at Columbia University, received his B.A. from Columbia College and his M.A. and Ph.D. from Harvard University, where he was a Teaching Fellow in Fine Arts. A consultant for "The World of Cézanne" in the TIME-LIFE Library of Art, Professor Reff is the editor of books on Klee and Picasso and the author of many articles on Cézanne and other 19th and 20th Century European artists.

On the Slipcase

Manet's boldly stroked pastel portrait of his friend George Moore, the English poet, painter, dramatist, art critic, is a masterly evocation of a bohemian personality. (Detail; see page 187 for full portrait.)

End Papers

Front: At the Café, an ink drawing by Manet, probably depicts the Café Guerbois, where, in the late 1860s, the artist and his friends met almost daily to drink and argue.
Back: With the greatest economy, Manet's agile pencil traces quick silhouettes and subtle shadows to reveal a small cluster of men and women in his drawing, *At the Theatre.*

TIME-LIFE BOOKS

EDITOR: Maitland A. Edey
Executive Editor: Jerry Korn
Text Director: Martin Mann
Art Director: Sheldon Cotler
Chief of Research: Beatrice T. Dobie
Picture Editor: Robert G. Mason
Assistant Text Directors: Harold C. Field, Ogden Tanner
Assistant Art Director: Arnold C. Holeywell
Assistant Chief of Research: Martha T. Goolrick

PUBLISHER: Rhett Austell
Associate Publisher: Walter C. Rohrer
Assistant Publisher: Carter Smith
General Manager: Joseph C. Hazen Jr.
Business Manager: John D. McSweeney
Production Manager: Louis Bronzo

Sales Director: Joan D. Manley
Promotion Director: Beatrice K. Tolleris
Managing Director, International: John A. Millington

TIME-LIFE LIBRARY OF ART

SERIES EDITOR: Robert Morton
Associate Editor: Diana Hirsh
Editorial Staff for *The World of Manet:*
Text Editor: Harvey B. Loomis
Picture Editor: Jane Scholl
Designer: Paul Jensen
Staff Writers: Tony Chiu, James MaHood,
Paula Norworth, Lucille Schulberg,
Peter Yerkes
Chief Researcher: Martha T. Goolrick
Researchers: Lynda Kefauver, Gail Hansberry Mattox,
Patricia Maye, Suzanne Seixas, Susanna Seymour
Art Assistant: Mervyn Clay

EDITORIAL PRODUCTION
Color Director: Robert L. Young
Assistant: James J. Cox
Copy Staff: Marian Gordon Goldman,
Laurie LaMartine, Florence Keith
Picture Department: Dolores A. Littles,
Suzanne Jaffe, Barbara S. Simon
Traffic: Arthur A. Goldberger

The following individuals and departments of Time Inc. helped to produce this book: Editorial Production, Robert W. Boyd Jr.; Editorial Reference, Peter Draz; Picture Collection, Doris O'Neil; Photographic Laboratory, George Karas; TIME-LIFE News Service, Richard M. Clurman; Correspondents Maria Vincenza Aloisi (Paris), Margot Hapgood (London), Mary Johnson (Stockholm), Elisabeth Kraemer (Bonn), Robert Kroon (Geneva), Traudl Lessing (Vienna) and Ann Natanson (Rome).

Contents

6

I

The Reluctant Revolutionary

Shortly after Édouard Manet's death, his friend, the painter Edgar Degas, remarked: "We did not know that he was this great." The comment is understandable: Manet the man had hidden Manet the artist; the removal of the former suddenly revealed the latter with utmost clarity.

Greatness can be either conservative or radical: in Manet's case it was the latter. On that point, minds as far apart as the esoteric poet Stéphane Mallarmé and the popular novelist Émile Zola, both Manet's contemporaries, agreed. The former described Manet as "the only man who tried to open up a new path for himself and for all painting"; the latter called him a "regenerator." Artists are seldom kind to colleagues, and Paul Cézanne was anything but attracted to Manet's personality, yet he declared that with him began "a new state of painting." As for Paul Gauguin, he said flatly, "Painting begins with Manet." Not since Giotto had an artist so truly deserved the epithet revolutionary. Indeed, it was the state of painting instigated by Giotto in the 14th Century, often modified but never basically questioned, that Manet overthrew, creating a new one: modern painting.

What was the revolution about? A picture by Manet, *Before the Mirror (pages 9-11)* says it better than words. A woman, half-dressed, probably young and possibly of easy virtue, her back to the viewer, is inspecting herself in a large mirror. The attitude is almost as familiar to painters as it is to women. Because art itself is a mirror held up to the world, the mirrors depicted by artists in their works are in a sense symbols of their profession. They reflect not only the model represented, but also the art of painting. Consider, for example, *Las Meninas*, by Manet's favorite artist, Velázquez. In this multiple portrait of the Spanish Royal Family almost everybody is looking at the two chief members of the household, the King and Queen. They, however, are only indirectly visible—in the mirror. It is as if the artist is telling us that painting is so faithful a reflection that the borderline between reality and art has been erased.

For centuries artists basically shared the view that the function of a painting was to mirror a model. The picture's meaning was the subject's meaning, and the more faithfully it mirrored a subject, the better the picture was. We become aware of a mirror only when it has a flaw. Hence, in the traditional view, painting should be smooth, impersonal; it must make its model visible, but not be visible itself.

When we turn to Manet's picture, we discover something very strange: what we see in the mirror is not the young woman's likeness but a bevy of brushstrokes, loosely knit, rough, thick—we see paint. Here is the sign of a rebellion so momentous that it was to transform the course of art: since the Renaissance, even since the late Middle Ages, painting had been content to represent the subject; henceforth it would demand to present itself, to exist on its own. In 1890, more than a decade after Manet painted *Before the Mirror*, the artist Maurice Denis summed up this drastic reversal of priorities in the relationship between the subject depicted and the act of depicting: "Remember that a picture—before being a war horse, a nude woman, or an anecdote—is essentially a plane surface covered with colors assembled in a certain order." This revolution was brought about by Manet.

Nobody was ever more miscast than Édouard Manet in the part of revolutionary. In one of their frequent quarrels, Degas snapped at his friend: "I have long known how much of a bourgeois you are!" Manet was exactly that, to the tip of his suede-gloved fingers. There was nothing of the stereotype artist about him. In dress, tastes, type of friends and way of life, even in outlook, he was every bit a part of the well-to-do upper-middle class into which he was born.

Amiable *boulevardiers* are seldom given to setting time bombs. Can Manet's friends be blamed for not taking the explosive nature of his art seriously? A man of Manet's class, background and means might, perhaps, become a good amateur painter—not a revolutionary. Manet himself was not happy in his provocative role, nor did he fully understand it. He pined for official acclaim and was honestly puzzled by its continued denial. He envied the successful society painters who were adulated by wealthy patrons. But despite great effort, he was unable to paint like the popular artists. A friend once saw Manet begin a young lady's portrait, determined that it should be as slick and prettified as those executed by the fashionable society painter, Charles-Josuah Chaplin. Bent on gathering all the aces in his hand, Manet made her wear her most delicate clothes, surrounded her with roses. Yet as he labored at the canvas, scraping, erasing, starting again, the picture became more and more brutal, till at last his friend exclaimed, "It's a crow! How hard you are on women!" Manet was in fact the reluctant victim of his genius. It took another genius, the poet Charles Baudelaire, to diagnose the compulsion that occasionally made Manet's rosy damsels turn into crows: "M. Manet, whom people think raving mad, is simply a very loyal, very simple man, who does all he can to be reasonable, but who unfortunately is marked from birth by romanticism."

Few artists have been so misunderstood, by others and by himself, as Manet. Small wonder: as a man he was Dr. Jekyll; as a painter, Mr. Hyde. Often attacked for the wrong reasons, he sometimes was acclaimed—but not for the right ones. Those who were shocked by the

Before the Mirror, 1876

Self-Portrait, 1879

work misjudged the man; those who knew the man could not imagine him capable of provoking an artistic revolution.

Édouard Manet was born in Paris on January 23, 1832. A younger brother, Eugène, born two years later, became a civil servant; a third brother, Gustave, born in 1835, became a prison inspector. Édouard was slated to be a lawyer. The cradle may seem an inappropriate place in which to determine a man's career, but Édouard's father, Auguste, was not the sort who left anything to improvisation. In the Manet family, the sons had been men of law for generations. Auguste spent his whole life in the civil service, gradually rising to high rank in the Ministry of Justice and ending his career as a judge. The role suited him ideally: he was a man of duty, sternly honest, unflaggingly virtuous. He was enormously self-righteous: a confirmed republican, he quarreled with his wife's brother, Edmond Fournier, because the latter, a monarchist, resigned from the army in 1848 out of loyalty to the dethroned King Louis-Philippe; the political argument capped a long series of disagreements between the two men, and Auguste, it is said, never saw his brother-in-law again.

Auguste's life was a web of inexorable routines. Twice a week he held receptions, not because he was sociable, but because it was expected of a well-salaried civil servant. He had inherited from his father 150 acres of valuable land in Gennevilliers, a northern suburb of Paris; there were some houses on the land, and in one of them—Gennevilliers was located on the river Seine, near Argenteuil—the family spent the summer holidays. The sobriety of the Manet home, therefore, was not a sign of impecuniousness but of the master's puritanism. At 19, his son was still not allowed to go out at night, and until his father's death, Édouard practically never missed a meal at home. Needless to say, Auguste Manet had as much whimsy and humor as a clock.

It was a clock, however, that symbolized the element of fantasy and warmth in the Manet home—a clock given by Charles XIV, King of Sweden, to Eugénie Fournier when she married Auguste Manet. The Fournier side of Manet's family was quite a different matter from his father's side. Eugénie's father was a bankrupt businessman and self-styled diplomat who had helped engineer the election of Charles, formerly Marshal Bernadotte in Napoleon's army, to the Swedish throne. In appreciation for Fournier's services, King Charles consented to be Eugénie's godfather—hence the wedding gift.

Eugénie herself was a woman of considerable imagination and artistic talent. Madame Manet loved music; she had a good voice and liked to use it. She delighted in receptions—her own and those of her well-bred friends—and often sang at them. It was she, no doubt, who insisted that her sons be given piano lessons, and to the end of his life, the painter was to count musicians such as Emmanuel Chabrier among his dearest friends. It is not farfetched to suppose that later on, when Édouard's artistic inclinations aroused his father's outraged protests, his mother, although openly espousing her husband's views, was secretly on her son's side.

But the threat of art had not yet arisen in the Manet home. At the age of 12, after a brief sojourn in a school run by a priest, Édouard Manet became a student at the Collège Rollin, a secondary institution set up in a former girls' reformatory. To young Manet, it undoubtedly seemed a prison still. "This child is feeble," the headmaster noted on Édouard's report card, "but he shows zeal, and we hope he will do well." A few years later, the child was still feeble but the zeal had slackened, and the reports describe him as being "distracted," "slightly frivolous" and "not very studious." Indeed, the only subject that he seems to have excelled in was athletics. Had his father not been a respected public figure and a friend of the school's director, Édouard would have flunked out. But in a bourgeois world where diplomas made the man, his father saw to it that Édouard was reprieved year after year, and he seemed slated to graduate, like many another mediocre son of a "good family," to a predestined career and an uneventful life of comfort.

Something utterly unforeseeable upset Auguste Manet's plans for his son. The provocation came—one might have guessed it—from the Fournier side. Mrs. Manet's brother Edmond was not only an army officer, but a passionate lover of art and an enthusiastic draftsman as well. He quickly realized that his nephew, too, had a passion for and a way with the pencil. The Collège Rollin offered an optional course in drawing: uncle Fournier suggested that Édouard register for it. The latter agreed enthusiastically, but Manet *père*, outraged by this new symptom of frivolity on his son's part, refused to pay the extra fee; so Colonel Fournier did (thereby sowing the seed of bitter discord that eventually separated the brothers-in-law). Manet's experience in the drawing class was, in a way, a prefiguration of his future troubles: no sooner had he joined it than he was suspended for a month for having sketched his neighbors rather than the proposed subject, a model wearing a helmet as in classical pictures. After the punishment was lifted, Manet soon became as proficient in drawing as in calisthenics.

This, however, was not another escape from the boredom of studies; it proved to be a deep-rooted commitment. It had to be to give the 16-year-old Édouard, a loving son accustomed to tremble before his father and to obey him, the courage to announce that he would not become a lawyer but a painter. Manet *père* fulminated, Manet *fils* trembled but did not give in. At last a compromise of sorts was struck: Édouard would become neither a lawyer nor a painter but a naval officer. In 1848 he left the Collège to prepare for his entrance examination to the naval school, and failed. Unsuccessful candidates were given another chance provided they spent six months on a training vessel. So in December he set sail for Brazil on the merchant ship *Le Havre et Guadeloupe*. At the beginning he was enthusiastic, but after some days at sea he wrote his mother, "What a monotonous life, this sailor's life. Always the sky and the water, always the same thing: it's stupid." Of course, he had not left his pencils behind; the captain, informed of his talent, is said to have shown him a shipment of Dutch cheeses whose red rinds had been discolored by the salty air and told him, "Since you are an artist, brighten up those cheeses." Yet neither the small pleasure of being appointed the ship's drawing instructor nor the excitement of exotic lands recon-

It is ironic that this portrait of Manet's parents should have been one of the first of his canvases to be accepted for exhibition at the official Salon—his father had objected strenuously to his becoming an artist in the first place. Though conventional enough to impress members of the Salon jury of 1861, the work, with its bold contrasts of light and dark, foreshadows the harsh, flat light in some of Manet's later pictures. The painting flouted tradition by making no effort to flatter. As a friend of the artist's remarked, "They might well be two concierges."

ciled Manet to the sailor's life. In June 1849 he was back home, perfunctorily failed his naval examination again, and told his father that this time nothing would stop him from becoming a painter.

While Manet was performing his private coup d'état, a public one was in the making. A revolution had taken place in France a few months before Manet went to sea in 1848. After two days of popular insurrection—during the night of February 24 alone, nearly 1,600 barricades were built in the streets of Paris—Louis-Philippe, the last of France's kings, was overthrown. Under him the new power of the 19th Century, the bourgeoisie, had come to the forefront. To the bourgeoisie Louis-Philippe had seemed the very incarnation of itself: his manners were very simple and affable, his appearance was plain and unheroic, his pear-shaped head was the cartoonist's delight. His selfishness and greed, too, were understandable traits. Age, however, had turned the "citizen king" into a despot; and the bourgeoisie was feeling its strength. "Get rich," his prime minister, Guizot, had urged the middle class. It had. So much so, in fact, that by mid-century it felt ready to take the reins of government into its own hands.

Yet economic liberalism, which created the new bourgeois fortunes, also resulted in increased poverty for most other Frenchmen. At this time, 26 million Frenchmen out of 31 million lived on less than 55 centimes—not quite the cost of a loaf of bread—a day. The impact of the Industrial Revolution, just beginning in France, led to the emergence of another new political force: the working class. Louis-Philippe had grossly underrated the strength of these two oppositions—the prosperous liberal bourgeoisie and the famished working people stirred by socialist thinkers. In 1848 the crisis that had been brewing came to a head in the February insurrection. Louis-Philippe fled Paris and went into exile in England.

The bourgeoisie and the working class had been united in battle. Now their aims began to diverge: the former wanted a conservative republic, the latter a progressive democracy. The working-class ideas prevailed at first. On February 25, Paris had awakened bedecked with red flags. Under the pressure of the militant masses, a provisional government took a series of bold social measures, such as providing universal employment. By April, however, the popular impetus was sagging and the bourgeoisie recovering its courage. Furthermore, Paris was not France; the country's predominantly rural population was terrified by the red flags. At the end of April, elections were held. Under Louis-Philippe only 200,000 people had the right to vote; now the entire male population—nine million persons—was called to the polls. A radical regime had grown out of street fighting; a conservative republic was born in the ballot boxes. The epilogue was inevitable: a desperate uprising of the workers on June 23 was brutally crushed; 11,000 people were arrested; many were imprisoned and deported. "Only the name Republic remained," mourned a contemporary socialist writer, Louis Blanc.

A mock republic was bound to have a president who made mockery of it. One of the representatives to the constitutional assembly elected in April 1848 was Charles-Louis-Napoleon Bonaparte. He was the third son of Napoleon's brother Louis and the flighty Hortense de Beauharnais (so flighty, in fact, that there is doubt about Louis-Napoleon's legitimacy). From adolescence, he had dreamed of restoring his uncle's Empire. Twice he had sought to overthrow Louis-Philippe, but his pronunciamentos had failed to arouse support for his ambitions.

Now he felt his hour had come. The provisional government was too weak to prevent him from taking his seat in the assembly, although when he announced his candidacy for the presidency, there were many who sensed the threat to the young, shaky republic. They knew that for Bonaparte the presidency was merely a stepping-stone to the imperial throne, but no one could stop Louis-Napoleon's progress. He was elected Prince-President, as he insisted on being addressed, just one day after Manet sailed for South America on his naval voyage. From Rio de Janeiro the young man, whose republican sentiments had led him to roam the streets excitedly during the February uprising, wrote to a cousin in France: "What do you say about the nomination of Louis-Napoleon? Above all do not name him emperor; it would be too funny."

It was only too serious. The Prince-President lost no time in securing control of the army, and he soon dropped every pretense of democratic procedure. With supreme arrogance he declared that "the name Napoleon is in itself a program." The coup d'état that, in December 1851, gave Louis-Napoleon control of France came as a surprise to no one; a year later he proclaimed himself Emperor Napoleon III. "Napoleon the Little," as Victor Hugo called him, promptly had the motto "Liberty, Equality, Fraternity" wiped off all public buildings because, in the terms of the Emperor's decree, "these three words have appeared only in times of turmoil and civil war: their rough inscription on our public edifices saddens and worries passersby." After less than four years, France had traded one form of authoritarianism for another.

The same fate befell Manet. He had hated school and deserted it for art, but art led him right back to school. And once again he ran afoul of his father's sense of propriety. Manet *père*, trying to salvage what could be salvaged, suggested to his son that he sign up at the École des Beaux-Arts (here, too, M. Manet had friends who would make things easy). The École, run by the Institut de France, which served as the government's cultural ministry, was the gateway to an almost respectable career. You enrolled in the École and entered one of the studios run by academic artists, members of the Institut; you tried to flatter your teacher enough to have him exert his influence on your behalf in the competition for the Prix de Rome; as a winner you returned from your sojourn in Rome and painted a picture or two that you submitted to the jury of the biennial Salon; sooner or later, you won a medal at the Salon and commissions started to come your way; by and by, you would obtain wealth, the Legion of Honor and election to the Institut. No wonder the successful artists of the time looked as solid and dignified as the bankers and industrialists whom they portrayed.

Manet's friend Claude Monet attended the studio of the academic artist Charles Gleyre, and he has left us his memories of it. During life classes, Monet recalled, Gleyre would move from easel to easel, correcting the students' work. Once when Monet sketched the model as he saw him, doing full justice to his enormous feet, Gleyre had shuddered with horror and told him, "Remember, young man, that . . . one must always think of antiquity. Nature, my friend, is good as a tool for study, but it is of no interest. Style, you see, is the thing that matters." And style was what the École tried to teach. Art critic Charles Blanc, an acquaintance of Manet's father, summarized what was meant by style: "The art of idealizing the true, of simplifying the spectacles of nature and dignifying them by bringing them together in a strong unity."

Real life could be used as raw material—although historical subjects were decidedly preferable—but only if its rawer side had been shunned and if the rest had been further filtered by translation into forms derived from the art of the ancients and of the Renaissance painters. If you wanted to depict a contemporary figure, you had, so to speak, to make him wear a toga; if he couldn't or wouldn't, you had to forego showing him. It was a sterilizing procedure, bound to produce monotonously impersonal, smoothly executed and uniformly conventional works. So much the better: the academics wholeheartedly subscribed to the precept of the German neoclassical theorist Johann Joachim Winckelmann: "Perfect beauty is like pure water: it has no particular taste." What the École taught, in short, was a more sophisticated version of the instruction provided by Manet's drawing class at the Collège Rollin: it was all classical helmets and no living neighbors.

Perhaps that is why Manet again defied his father by refusing to join the École des Beaux-Arts; he turned instead for instruction to Thomas Couture, whose studio he entered in January 1850, at the age of 18. Couture had scored a fabulous hit with his colossal canvas, *The Romans of the Decadence*. "At last France has her own Veronese!" the critics rejoiced. The cascades of praise showered on Couture went to his head. "I pride myself in the belief that I am the only truly serious artist of our epoch," he boasted. Ingres, Delacroix? Pygmies next to him. And to give young painters the benefit of his genius, he opened his own art

Manet's teacher, Thomas Couture, made a great success at the Salons with pictures like *The Romans of the Decadence (below)*, in which the musky air of eroticism is sanitized by a strong breath of moral disapproval. Couture knew he could titillate his audience with a frank orgy and yet bring the picture within the bounds of acceptability by revealing that *he* knew, and that he was aware his audience knew, just how decadent this ancient group was. He shows it by including in the sensual scene figures intended to convey disapproval: statues of the heroic ancestors of these lewd Romans as well as the fully clothed poet and philosopher at right. Meticulously painted from carefully posed models, Couture's huge canvas—it is about 15 by 25 feet—is typical of the academic style which Manet rejected.

school. Twice a week he would inspect the work of his pupils, comment on it, roll a cigarette and tell stories of his own student days.

But at heart, Couture's teaching differed little from the doctrine of the École—"idealism and impersonality" was his motto—and Manet's disenchantment began the day he entered his studio. He was given a plaster cast of an ancient sculpture to sketch. After turning it round and round, he sketched it upside down. "It seemed more interesting that way." Manet's irritation grew with time. "I don't know why I am here," he told a friend. "Everything we are given to look at is ridiculous. The light is false, the shadows are false. When I arrive at the studio, I feel as if I were entering a tomb." He flew into rages at models who posed—as they had been taught to do—like classical statues. Once he railed at Dubosc, a model celebrated for his truly heroic attitudes. Indignant, Dubosc exclaimed: "M. Manet, thanks to me more than one young man has painted compositions that led him to Rome." "We are not in Rome and we don't want to go there," Manet retorted. "We are in Paris, let's stay here."

The young man passionately meant what he said. He loved his city and its boulevards, cafés, double-decker horse-drawn omnibuses, its fashionable carriages and elegant women. During the 1850s Paris was remodeled by Baron Georges Eugène Haussmann, who laid out straight, spacious boulevards through the old tortuous capital, and Manet watched the massive reconstruction with avid interest. "Paris has never known a *flâneur* [stroller] like him," wrote one of the artist's oldest friends, Antonin Proust. From the chic garden of the Tuileries to the sordid slum called "Little Poland," Manet walked and observed, indefatigable, taking advantage of the many newly built sidewalks. (Their construction may partly account for the extraordinary increase in streetwalkers, whose vast numbers did much to earn Paris the name of "modern Babylon.")

The trouble was that Manet loved art, but loved life just as well—and the two seemed utterly antithetical. Couture's predominant concern with the former and Manet's interest in the latter clashed again and

In two hectic decades, Paris was transformed from a jumble of haphazard streets into an orderly metropolis under the guiding hand of Baron Georges Eugène Haussmann, who was given the job of beautifying the city by Napoleon III in the early 1850s. These two views of the Île de la Cité, an island in the Seine, suggest the extent of the rebuilding. In a topographical drawing of 1739 *(above)*, the Cathedral of Notre Dame is surrounded by slums. Haussmann proposed the Île as a site for important municipal buildings; the slums were razed and, as shown in the 1867 photograph below, a new city hospital was built in their place.

again. Once, taking advantage of the fact that his teacher had not yet arrived, Manet ordered a male model to pose in his street clothes before the class. When Couture came in, he exploded: "Do you pay Gilbert not to be naked? Who is responsible for this silly idea?" Incidents such as this occurred so frequently that in 1853 Manet took a leave of absence from Couture's studio and went to Italy. He visited Venice and spent some time in Florence, dutifully copying works by Titian, Fra Angelico and other Renaissance masters.

If master and pupil had hoped that his contact with these revered artists would exorcise the mischievous spirits that plagued Manet, they were soon disappointed. Back in Couture's studio, the frictions promptly arose again. Manet was angry with his master for not providing him with the formula that would enable him to reconcile style and life, and his frustration drove him to outbursts and demonstrations of ill humor that disruptively fascinated his fellow students. For several years the feud dragged on; one day, after Couture had commented unfavorably upon Manet's study of Marie, a red-haired model, the other students, disagreeing, ostentatiously applauded Manet and wreathed his easel with flowers. "My friend," said Couture, "if you have the pretension of being the leader of a school, go and found it elsewhere."

But becoming the leader of a school of painting was no easy matter. Despite his dissatisfaction with his academic instruction, Manet found it almost impossible to break away from the tyranny of the past. At mid-19th Century, the two most powerful creative figures in French art were still Ingres and Delacroix, both well over 50. Their feud had been dominating the French scene for more than a quarter of a century. Delacroix sarcastically described Ingres as "narrow-minded" and "Chinese" (in the sense of "finicky"), while Ingres called Delacroix "the apostle of ugliness" and "the drunken broom." It was a battle of titans in which Delacroix stood for warm color and romantic passion, while Ingres represented coolness of line and classical serenity. Their originality set them apart from their contemporaries. The academics resented their genius with all the spitefulness of mediocrity, and even their own admirers and disciples could produce only pale, lifeless imitations.

With these masters shut up in proud isolation, there were very few examples of genius to inspire a novice looking for a way to break from the past. One early rebel against authority was Honoré Daumier, son of a workman, who raised caricature to the status of a major art form. An infallible gift for the telling line, a caustic sense of observation and a deep love of liberty and of the underdog found expression in some 4,000 lithographs ranging from political satire to social comedy. Daumier's very success, however, spoiled his career as a painter. When censorship introduced by Napoleon III gagged him after 1852, he sought an outlet in painting. Yet although he executed some 200 canvases (pages 47-49), whose bold approach provided a moving expression of the city and of its victims, not even his admirers took his paintings seriously, regarding them instead as the private hobby of a formidable journalist. (Indeed, Couture, in a moment of exasperation, once chided Manet for his interest in contemporary subjects by saying, "My poor fellow, you will never be more than the Daumier of your time.")

A far more devastating and effective assault on traditionalism was launched by the self-styled—rightly so—creator of Realism, Gustave Courbet. However, his unflattering, beefy renditions of peasant life did not attract widespread public attention until the very year, 1850, that saw Manet enter on an artistic career. But it was still too early for the young man to understand that Courbet was turning a page in the history of French art and pointing the way for the next generation of innovators, of whom he, Manet, was to be the leader.

The only direction in which a young artist in search of fresh inspiration might have looked at the time was toward the landscapists. Around 1830 a handful of artists had begun to realize that looking at nature was the best way to become more natural. About 1836 Théodore Rousseau settled at Barbizon, on the edge of the forest of Fontainebleau, a locale that offered a host of picturesque vistas; he was joined by Narcisse Diaz, Charles François Daubigny and Jean-François Millet *(page 46)*. But though they sought new insights through the direct observation of nature, Rousseau and his companions of the Barbizon School remained, to a large extent, contaminated by the sentimental or rhetorical formulas of the academic tradition.

Perhaps the only landscapist to free himself from these vices was Corot. The simplicity, sincerity and exquisite transparency of his paintings are the esthetic counterparts of a goodness of character that bordered on saintliness (his charity led him to sign his name to a number of landscapes by students who thus could sell them at a better price). Modesty was one side of the coin, boldness the other. "Don't imitate, don't follow the others, or else you will lag behind them," said Corot. His long visits to Italy provided his landscapes with their solid, underlying geometry; the subtleties of the skies of Ile-de-France—he settled at Ville d'Avray, a wooded, pond-studded suburb of Paris—encouraged his penchant for hazy atmospheres and delicate values. In his best landscapes *(page 45)*, solid structure and subtle ambience are combined with a mastery born of utter candor.

These canvases were studies, however—works for private consumption. Not until 1849 did Corot exhibit one of them at the Salon, for pure landscape, unidealized and lacking human figures, was considered uninteresting by the Salon juries. So, Corot's public reputation was built on the least original part of his work: "historical" landscapes.

Hence the novice Manet was not really exposed to pure landscape. Even if he had been, it is unlikely that he would have succumbed to its seductions. Manet was a man of the city, not of the country, and for him—as for the overwhelming majority of the art public—serious painting meant figure painting. Thus, wherever he looked, he saw little but inflated nonentities who practiced historical or genre painting, offering budding artists a sterile choice between classical idealism and romantic idealism.

Even conservative critics agreed that a low-water mark in French painting had been reached. "Today art has at its disposal only dead ideas and formulas which no longer correspond to its needs," wrote art critic and poet Théophile Gautier in 1853. He concluded: "It is well known that something must be done—but what?" (The same note had been sounded for France as a whole by Victor Hugo when he lamented, after the revolution of 1848, "Poor great nation, unconscious and blind! It knows what it does not want, but it does not know what it wants.") Still another poet, Charles Baudelaire, who was also the most original art critic of his time, summed up the problem succinctly: "The grand tradition is lost and the new one is not yet created." As early as 1845 he had expressed this fervent wish: "May the real explorers give us next year the rare joy of hailing the advent of the *new!*"

The stage was set; however, Manet was far from ready to make his appearance. He had spent six years in Couture's school, yet produced few paintings aside from copies. Like Gautier, he could ask the crucial question, but not answer it. "I hate what is useless," he confided to Proust, "but the deuce is to see that only which is useful. The tricks-of-the-trade of painting have perverted us. How shall we get rid of them? Who will deliver us from the overelaborate?" Even his break with Couture did not lead to the creation of original work; he continued, for several years, to submit his pictures for his erstwhile master's approval. Obviously, despite his differences with Couture, Manet wished to rebel against him no more than he had wanted to disobey his father.

BIBLIOTHÈQUE NATIONALE, PARIS

The influential critic and poet Charles Baudelaire, shown here in an etching by Manet, did much to encourage the artist in the early 1860s. He was one of the first to praise Manet's works publicly, and though 11 years older, with eccentric habits and exotic tastes, he became a close friend of the painter. They habitually dined together in Paris' elegant restaurants, and Baudelaire often accompanied Manet on sketching expeditions to the Tuileries Garden. The association was short-lived, however, for the poet died in 1867 at age 46, from the ruinous effects of drugs, alcohol and syphilis.

The solution to his dilemma was simple, really. As Manet himself put it to Proust: "There is only one true thing: instantly paint what you see. When you've got it, you've got it. When you haven't, you begin again. All the rest is humbug." But it was one thing to say it, another to do it. Some early sketches may perhaps have fit this description, but only because they were, in the artist's own eyes, inconsequential doodles in the margins of his artistic quest. To be meaningful, the program would have to be carried out on the ground on which Manet decided to stand or fall: figure painting. And here, he was paralyzed. For style, that degenerate version of the tradition taught by the École, was like an old man's stomach: it could no longer digest the rich fare of contemporary reality—the new way of life that was pulsing through the changing 19th Century society. To paint it, one would have to work outside the tradition, an act of revolt so rare that it would have intimidated a far more aggressive personality than Manet.

His hesitations, the slowness of his progress—despite a painterly skill that everybody recognized almost from the outset—were due to his refusal to take the plunge and, unmindful of convention, to paint what he saw as he saw it. Instead, he hedged, compromised, strove to formulate the stuff of life in terms of the museum. In the Louvre, that formidable storehouse of the Grand Tradition, Manet hoped to find the solution to his problems. "The Louvre! The Louvre! There is only the Louvre. You can never make too many copies!" once urged the painter Fantin-Latour, whom Manet met and befriended in those hallowed halls. It was here, too, that he met a young man engaged in drawing an *Infanta* by Velázquez directly on the etching plate. "What gumption! You'll be lucky if you carry it off!" exclaimed Manet. The young man introduced himself: his name was Degas.

Manet copied works by Fra Angelico and Boucher, Titian and Rembrandt; he even visited Delacroix to ask him for permission to copy his famous work, *Bark of Dante*. The grand old man of Romanticism agreed, urging him to study Rubens "who," he said, "is god." Manet's god was not to be the exuberant Flemish painter, but he did find a master who led him at least partway toward the goal he sought. About 1855 he copied Velázquez' *Little Cavaliers* (ironically, the picture is now attributed not to the 17th Century Spanish master but to his son-in-law Mazo). "Ah, that's clean," he exclaimed in praise of the Spaniard's work. "How one is disgusted with the stews and gravies!" Abrupt handling of color, rough, starkly juxtaposed brushstrokes, dramatic contrast—Velázquez' boldness and freedom were the antidote Manet needed against the smooth brushwork, the dull finish, the plodding, mechanical gradations, the "brown gravy" extolled by the École.

Inspired by this powerful stimulus, Manet produced in 1858-1859 the first picture he ever sent to the Salon, *The Absinthe Drinker (page 29)*. (It was not accepted for the exhibition, although Delacroix, with his penetrating eye, voted for its admission.) This canvas marks the end of Manet's apprentice years—he showed it to Couture, who greeted it with a sarcastic, "The only drunkard is you," whereupon the incensed young artist shouted, "It is all over!" and broke off relations with him. Significantly, Manet's model for the picture was a ragpicker—one of thousands who plied their trade in Paris and who constituted one of the notable realities of the time. It is fitting that Manet found his ragpicker at the Louvre, where he had also found Velázquez.

Speaking of the picture, Manet explained what Velázquez had brought him: "I painted a Parisian character whom I had studied in Paris, and I executed it with the technical simplicity I discovered in Velázquez." Here, at last, was a way out of the dilemma: Manet's contemporaries fitted into Velázquez' clothes. The first canvas in which he fully resorted to this formula was *The Guitar Player* of 1860. It was one of the first two of his works to be accepted at the Salon in 1861 (the other was a portrait of his parents), and it won an honorable mention.

Throughout most of the next decade, Manet applied the recipe again and again. He used Spanish models, such as the members of the visiting ballet company of the Royal Theater of Madrid, or he dressed up as matadors Parisians like his brother Gustave or Victorine Meurend—a girl whom he had accosted in the street and who quickly became his favorite sitter. Baudelaire was quite right in noting that, with Manet, "the genius of Spain seems to have taken refuge in France."

Long ignored, Spanish culture had become of increasing interest to the French in recent decades. The Romantic painters and writers, with their thirst for color, passion and drama, seized upon it. Victor Hugo, Théophile Gautier, Alexandre Dumas made it one of their favorite themes. In 1838 a famous art collection assembled by King Louis-Philippe and called the "Spanish Museum," was opened to the public, who thus grew familiar with the work of Zurbarán, Murillo, Velázquez and Goya. Another wave of hispanomania was set off by Napoleon III's marriage, in 1853, to a beautiful young Spanish woman, Eugénie de

Montijo. The Empress danced the fandango, played the castanets and, at the inauguration of the Longchamp race track, remarked to the Duc de Morny, who had conceived and fashioned this essential cog in the machinery of *la vie parisienne,* "Confess, my dear Prince, that your races aren't worth a good bullfight."

The French public would seem therefore to have been prepared for Manet's *guitarreros, majas* and matadors *(pages 32-33).* And yet there was in his Spanish pictures a disturbing element, a jarring note for which the public, no matter how much exposed to the Spanish school, was not ready. When they saw *The Guitar Player,* a group of very young artists, including Fantin-Latour, were so struck by the "strange new way" in which it was painted that in a body they paid Manet an admiring visit. Most observers were not so complimentary; for some, the newness came as a blow. One visitor to Manet's first one-man exhibition at the Galerie Martinet in 1863 threatened to hit back with his walking stick at one of the paintings displayed. "It was brutal," noted a critic about Manet's way of painting. Even favorable judgments emphasized Manet's aggressiveness. "Imagine Goya transferred to Mexico, turned savage in the pampas and smearing canvases with crushed cochineal, and you have M. Manet," wrote an observer. "His pictures are splattered palettes. Never has anyone made lines grimace and colors shriek more horribly." Another critic, probably Delacroix writing anonymously, said, "His acid color penetrates the eye like a steel saw; his figures are hacked out with a rawness untempered by any compromise. He has all the sharpness of those green fruits which are fated never to ripen."

The effect of Manet's works was startling. It was as if he had removed from the viewers' noses the smoked glasses with which they were used to looking at paintings. What gave him this blinding force? Critics have suggested it was the brightness of his color, the starkness of his contrasts, and some still support this explanation. Yet the paintings of Manet around 1860 are not particularly bright; and though he relies on violent tonal effects, on the drama of black and white, he does so no more than Velázquez or Goya, whose pictures shocked few people. The difference lies elsewhere. Bold as they were, the Spaniards' works did not break from tradition; parts of Manet's pictures did. They did not remind his public of familiar forms. Until then, painting had used indirect discourse; Manet introduced direct discourse, an unheard-of immediacy. Instead of easing their reception through inclusion of familiar references and conventions, the figures in his paintings face us alone, as in *The Street Singer* with its haunting glimpse of a poor Paris girl, at once so alive and so vulnerable, stepping out of a cabaret. Her wan beauty is clearly threatened, limited to the shortest of spans by the consequences of her undernourished childhood and the exhaustion of hard work and sleepless nights; but the absence of the past and of a future gives her an almost overwhelming presence. Indeed, she is so very present because she is *only* of the present—and, as such, she may stand as the symbol and illustration of Manet's revolutionary contribution to art: the discovery of the present.

Manet achieved his first critical successes with a series of canvases on Spanish motifs. He later copied two of them, making the etching of *The Guitar Player* and a lithograph of *Lola de Valence* reproduced here. The guitarist was probably a Spanish model; Lola was the leading dancer of a touring Spanish dance troupe popular in Paris during the fall of 1862. Manet's painting inspired his friend Zacharie Astruc to write a song "Lola de Valence," and Manet made the lithograph to illustrate the sheet music.

The present does not explode at once and totally in Manet's painting. It appears first in minor details, such as the audience glimpsed through a jagged opening of the stage set in the background of *Lola de Valence.* Or it is restricted to a face, a single figure—and it is no coincidence that this figure often belonged to the model of *The Street Singer,* Victorine Meurend, whose looks were the typical product of the modern, industrial-age metropolis into which Paris was just developing.

Only once in those early years did Manet's sense of the present invade a large composition involving a number of figures: *Concert in the Tuileries (pages 30-31),* executed sometime between 1860 and 1862. Here at last was a picture that fulfilled his credo, "Instantly paint what you see." He had prepared himself for this ambitious work by a number of oil sketches done in the fashionable Tuileries garden. And what he saw—a crowd—was as new as the freshness of his approach—for crowds were a by-product of the recently born modern city just as surely as the frail face of Victorine Meurend was. In *Concert* a great assembly of dandies and chic women have clustered in what one may suppose to be the vicinity of the bandstand, and they chat while children play at their feet. One can almost hear the hum of conversation. this is the life Manet lived and loved; these faces are those of his contemporaries. Some are the people Paris was talking about—Jacques Offenbach, Théophile Gautier, Baron Taylor (who had helped Louis-Philippe build up his Spanish Museum); some are relatives and friends —his brother Eugène, Fantin-Latour; and there was Baudelaire, the friend whom he so admired and who had been among the first to detect the young painter's talent.

Indeed, many years before in a review of the Salon of 1845, Baudelaire had prayed for the advent of an artist capable of painting just such a picture as *Concert:* "Nobody lends an ear to the wind which will blow tomorrow; and yet the heroism of *modern life* surrounds and presses us . . . . He shall be the *painter,* the true painter, who will know how to extract from current life its epic side, and make us see and understand, by means of color and line, how great and poetic we are with our neckties and our varnished boots."

Yet Baudelaire, who wrote a quatrain in honor of Manet's *Lola de Valence,* never so much as mentioned the *Concert.* It was either ignored or attacked, despite the fact that it was the first truly modern picture, the first to embody fully what Baudelaire called the "essential quality of being present." Despite? More likely, because of it. It was too far ahead of its time. It was even ahead of Manet's development—it took him years to catch up with its modernity.

For Manet was a reluctant prophet. In a way he was as perturbed as the public by the insistent outpouring of the present from his brush. Even in later years, when he could no longer ignore the message of which he was the bearer, he still recoiled against the reckless strain in himself and produced pictures that were clearly intended to satisfy museum curators. The Manet vein in him was shocked by the Fournier vein and did its best to put it down; at nearly every turn of his career, reassuringly conservative pictures follow upon daring ones. Especially around 1860, when Manet, at 28, was in the early stages of his career, he was sincerely attached to the past, still doing his utmost to repress the breakthrough of the present in his painting. A picture called *Fishing in Saint-Ouen*, for instance, shows not only one of Manet's favorite promenades on the Seine, but the artist himself, together with a woman and a boy who, as we shall see, were of immediate importance to him. Such a large dose of actuality was too much: Manet disguised it in a composition borrowed from Rubens. The same compensatory reflex later made him cast the revolutionary message of *Olympia* in the familiar mold of Titian's *Venus of Urbino*.

This leaning on tradition did nothing to make Manet's painting more palatable to the public. In fact, it made his work even more shocking because the unmistakable element of the present in his pictures showed that the past *was* past. The conventions of the past were no longer able to express the urgency of the present. The two concepts seemed awkwardly juxtaposed or, worse still, entered into open conflict. Not surprisingly, the tension between past and present under which Manet was laboring at this time found expression in the picture on which he concentrated all his energies and which he was determined to make his *grande machine*, the masterpiece that would definitively establish his reputation: the picture now known as *Luncheon on the Grass (Déjeuner sur l'herbe) (pages 34-35)*. Its greatness lies in the absolute honesty with which it reflects the stress of Manet's Jekyll-and-Hyde duality. Indeed, this duality provides both the subject and the texture of *Luncheon*. In it, the breaking point is reached between tradition and originality, between past and present. The crack in the history of art, which was soon to grow so deep that pre-Manet and post-Manet painting would belong to irreconcilable worlds, becomes visible in this work.

It is hard to imagine a greater accumulation of rift-engendering contradictions. The idea of *The Bath*, as Manet himself called the huge canvas (it measures almost 7 feet by 9 feet), had come to him while looking at bathers in the Seine. He executed some sketches outdoors but painted the picture in his studio in such a way that the figures and the landscape appear painfully disconnected. He might have attenuated this disparity had the female nude been a conventional figure—say, a nymph—set against a conventional backdrop. Instead, Manet painted her in a contemporary manner that makes her look almost pasted onto the landscape; and the nonmythological nature of the girl is further accentuated by the unambiguously modern appearance of her two male companions: they are dressed like gentlemen of the 1860s. As a result, the girl is no longer a timeless nude but an undressed contemporary— and, of course, her white flesh and the men's dark costumes constitute the most startling contrast of all in this schizophrenic work.

There are other glaring breakdowns in the picture's continuity. As if to compensate for the modernity of his three models, Manet has arranged them in a composition that is copied from an engraving after Raphael's *Judgment of Paris (page 34)*; similarly, the startling contrast of dressed male and naked female figures was probably derived from Giorgione's *Fête Champêtre (page 34)*. Manet has posed real people in a tableau borrowed from the Renaissance tradition; and even if the viewer does not know this, he obscurely feels it, because of a certain stiffness and implausibility in the actors' attitudes and gestures.

The crevices, the disparateness manifest in the subject and general composition of *Luncheon on the Grass* occur also in the way it is painted. There is no common denominator to unify the contrast between the tight, thick brushwork of the naked girl and the loose strokes of her neighbors; between the freshness of the still life in the foreground and the almost ridiculously proplike artificiality of the bird suspended in the upper-middle distance; between the brutal studio light falling upon the central group and the delicate, Corotesque atmosphere of the landscape. Even in the landscape itself, Manet could not achieve a continuity of effect. Not only does it seem to belong to another painting than the foreground, but it is itself broken up into unrelated parts: the water of pond and river appears divided into three levels, and we feel tempted to shout to the girl wading in the distance, "Watch out for the rapids!" Thus, everything Manet did to resolve the contradictions created new ones. The work, which he intended as a grand reconciliation, turned, against his will, into a confession of incompatibility.

Men misunderstood it, but history did it full justice: *Luncheon on the Grass*, which marked the split between past and present in Manet's career, was the occasion of the divorce not only between independent artists and the academics, but also between the new art and the public.

In 1863 Manet submitted the recently completed *Luncheon* and two other pictures to the jury of the Salon. They were, predictably, vetoed. Police states are irresistibly attracted to police mentalities: the dictatorial Napoleon III placed the Salon in the hands of the reactionaries of the Institut. Year after year, their severity increased: out of 5,000 works submitted in 1863, 2,800 were refused by the jury. The outcry among artists was tremendous. It was all very well for the illustrious Ingres to snub the Salon and to describe it contemptuously as a "shop" —he could get away with it. But the trouble was that there *was* no other shop to speak of, for art galleries with changing exhibitions were extremely rare. The biennial Salon was an artist's only real contact with critics, public and collectors; his sustenance depended for the next two years on his being accepted. As late as 1881, Auguste Renoir noted: "There are barely 15 art lovers in Paris capable of liking an artist without the Salon. There are 80,000 of them who will not even buy a nose if the painter is not in the Salon." One can understand why one young painter, upon learning that his pictures had been refused, committed suicide. So important was this vexatious institution to the artists of the time that Fantin-Latour, who had become a recluse in his old age, would venture outside once a year: the day of the Salon opening.

In a sudden fit of liberalism, or in the secret hope of smothering the complainants under ridicule, Napoleon III ordered that the artists who had been turned down be allowed, if they so wished, to show their entries in a separate exhibition. Of the 2,000 artists excluded, fewer than half took up the challenge; among them were Pissarro, Whistler, Fantin-Latour, Cézanne and Manet, whose three Salon submissions had

So many pictures were shown at the Paris Salons that, as this anonymous cartoon suggests, telescopes and ladders might have been valuable aids to the museum-goer. The great number of entries—as many as 5,000, pared down from perhaps 9,000 submissions —forced the Salon out of the Louvre in 1857 and into the larger Palace of Industry, built for the world exposition of 1855. There, in grimy, badly lighted rooms, pictures were hung floor to ceiling and so jammed together that one of the few ways an artist could ensure attention for his picture was to paint a canvas so large it could not be overlooked.

been vetoed. The Salon des Refusés, as this counter-salon came to be known, marks a capital date in the history of modern painting: henceforth the body artistic split into the "academics" and the "independents." The experiment of the Salon des Refusés was never to be forgotten by the revolutionary artists of later years. In 1863 the École's undisputed authority ended and the avant-garde was born.

The Salon opened, as usual, on May 1; the Salon des Refusés on May 15. The latter's success was immediate and enormous: 4,000 people visited it on a single Sunday. Yet it was certainly not the kind of success the artists had hoped for. Parisians rushed to it as to a slapstick comedy. "People entered it as they would the horror chamber at Madame Tussaud's in London," one *refusé* later recalled. "They laughed as soon as they had passed the door."

This reaction voiced an attitude of derision and insult on the part of the public toward innovators that has lasted to this day. Such lack of comprehension reflects the divorce between modern art and the modern audience, which took place at the same moment as the break between the École and the avant-garde. Indeed, the two events are intimately related. The bourgeoisie that made up the new public was, like all parvenus, devoid of artistic culture; incapable of reaching its own judgment, it clung frantically to whatever authority seemed available—and the only one was the Salon. Consequently, it espoused the cause of the École. Regrettable, but understandable. After all, it was not the bourgeoisie's fault that the tradition had dried up, that the common values, which had previously enabled artists and their societies to remain understandable to one another, had broken down, and that the academic artists were no longer able to incorporate the present into a stable, familiar framework. Inner necessity was driving the modern artist out on his solitary limb; could the public be blamed for not following him there?

Of the three Manet canvases on exhibition, *Luncheon on the Grass* at once attracted the most attention. It was hung in the farthest room, but, in the words of one reviewer, "it bored right through the wall." Speaking of Manet, a vanguard critic and friend of the artist called him "the dazzle, inspiration, piquancy, astonishment of the exhibition." In a way, the public agreed: Manet *was* the center of the Salon des Refusés. A veritable barrage of abuse and sarcasm was leveled at *Luncheon*. "Indecent" and "shocking" were among the gentlest of the epithets. "A commonplace woman of the demimonde, as naked as can be, shamelessly lolls between two dandies dressed to the teeth," ranted the journalist Louis Etienne. "This is a young man's practical joke, a shameful open sore not worth exhibiting." Even a well-disposed connoisseur like Thoré-Bürger wrote: "I can't imagine what made an artist of intelligence and refinement select such an absurd composition."

No wonder the majority of critics accused Manet of wanting deliberately to *épater le bourgeois* ("make the bourgeois gape"), of "having selected his subject in order to cause scandal." Indeed, the latter word comes up with revelatory frequency: Manet was the first modern artist to be the beneficiary—or the victim—of a *succès de scandale*.

A Notorious Debut

At the age of 27, Manet began painting the pictures that marked him as the most forceful and controversial artist of his generation. In 1859 he produced *The Absinthe Drinker (right)*, and from then on, although he turned out some perfectly conventional pictures and had a few accepted at the official Salon, the best of his work showed striking originality. These early masterpieces varied widely in subject and artistic approach, but most of them reflected Manet's interest in the contemporary scene— and all were either ignored or rejected by the art public.

The Absinthe Drinker shown at right, for example, was criticized because it made no effort to sentimentalize the subject's unsavory condition. Contemporary subjects were not in themselves taboo, but Manet's moody treatment, his indistinct outlines and background—in short, his unacademic approach—offended the public eye. Even when Manet, inspired by the works of Velázquez, painted a series of pictures with acceptable Spanish motifs, critics were still often put off by the eccentric coloring, by the flat perspective and by the contrasts between tradition and innovation that often found their way into his work. But in 1863, with *Luncheon on the Grass (pages 34-35)*, Manet went far beyond anything he had yet done to outrage his viewers. Their reaction is understandable perhaps—it is still a disquieting masterpiece—but the scandal was to shadow Manet for the rest of his career.

Manet departed from the academic practice of his day by using as his model for this picture not a professional but a ragpicker named Collardet, whom he encountered near the Louvre. He painted him in a pose—full length against a vague backdrop, with a still-life object on the ground—that was reminiscent of portraits by Velázquez. But the Salon jury to which Manet submitted the work in 1859 rejected it.

The Absinthe Drinker, 1858-1859

Concert in the Tuileries was one of the first pictures in which Manet expressed a fascination for his favorite milieu—a fashionable Paris gathering place crowded with elegant members of the social and artistic worlds. Here and there in this audience, shown listening to an unseen orchestra, Manet has painted recognizable portraits: the bearded dandy standing in profile at the center is Manet's brother Eugène; just behind him, against the tree, is the composer Jacques Offenbach; directly behind the young woman in a blue bonnet is the poet Charles Baudelaire in profile, and partly cut off at the extreme left is Manet himself.

A remarkably well-unified group portrait, *Concert* gives the impression of showing hundreds of persons in a small space without actually delineating all of them, and without looking cluttered. Manet has achieved this partly by composing the picture in a series of receding, increasingly darker horizontal planes. The sunlight illuminating the two women in the foreground gives way to a shadowy middle distance and finally to the density of the woods beyond. The small patch of blue sky is vital to the picture's sense of space—if one covers it, the foliage appears to crowd the picture oppressively.

Concert, which received little attention in Manet's time, is now seen as one of the first truly modern pictures in the sense that it straightforwardly shows a strictly contemporary moment without narrative or comment.

Concert in the Tuileries, 1860-1862

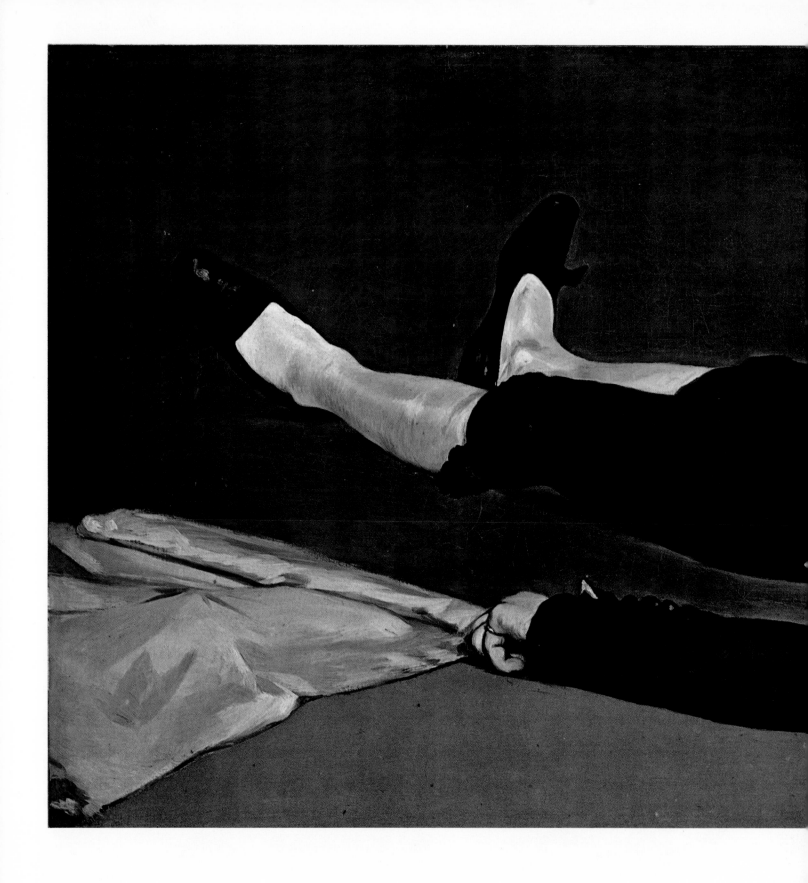

Manet's interest in Spanish painters such as Velázquez, Goya and Murillo led him to frequent use of Spanish themes in his early works. Some of these were praised and occasionally exhibited, but others were denounced for their innovations. Among the condemned was *The Dead Toreador (above)*, which was originally part of a larger work called *Incident in the Bull Ring*. In that picture the bull was so small in the background and the toreador lay so stiff in the foreground that one pundit said Manet had painted "a wooden toreador killed by a horned rat." Manet himself was unsatisfied with the picture, for he cut it up and threw away the offending bull.

What probably upset Manet's audience was his failure to exploit the dramatic possibilities of a gored bullfighter

The Dead Toreador, 1864

lying on the blood-soaked sand of a bull ring; Manet's matador looked more like a model lying on the studio floor. It was true that Manet was less interested in narrative than in achieving bold composition and coloring, which make the picture move in quite a different way. The foreshortening of the matador's body and the shallow, featureless background give the picture a flatness that thrusts the figure forward with a monumental presence. The flatness also emphasizes the purely visual pattern made by Manet's striking coloring. He had discovered the dramatic potential of black in Velázquez' work, and here he contrasts it starkly with olive, pink and brilliant white. This provocative use of black against color became a hallmark of Manet's early masterpieces.

33

Giorgione: *Fête Champêtre*, c.1505-1510

Marcantonio Raimondi engraving after Raphael: *The Judgment of Paris*, c.1525-1530

anet's *Luncheon on the Grass (right)* was his most controversial early picture, and yet in it he had borrowed heavily from tradition, chiefly that of 16th Century Italy. Giorgione's allegorical *Fête Champêtre (top)* gave him the idea of a nude female with clothed men. The group in the lower right corner of the engraving after Raphael's *Judgment of Paris (bottom)* apparently inspired the arrangement of Manet's three central figures. But these conventional elements did not appease Manet's audience, which was enraged by this 19th Century hussy, shamelessly nude, staring out from a scene full of curious inconsistencies. Later viewers, however, have found the painting to be an engrossing masterpiece. From the strangely mythological tone of the setting to the delicate realism of the foreground still life, the work is full of provocative images. Despite, or perhaps because of, its inscrutable aura, *Luncheon* has made an almost unforgettable impact on modern art.

Luncheon on the Grass (Déjeuner sur l'herbe), 1863

35

II

A Passion
for Reality

Manet's *Luncheon on the Grass* caused the first scandal of modern art, but he was by no means the first painter to scandalize the 19th Century. Fifteen years earlier the artistic establishment had been shaken up by the onslaught of another prime mover in art's transition from past to present, Gustave Courbet.

It is not surprising that Manet's friend Baudelaire, the most brilliant commentator on modernity of his time, was also a friend of Courbet— both painters had, in Baudelaire's words, "a decided taste for reality, modern reality." Unlike the well-bred Manet, Courbet also had a decided taste for scandal. In fact, he longed for the conflagration. "I painted this picture so it would be refused," he confided once, "and I succeeded." Whenever he became the center of controversy he would exclaim blissfully, "What a rumpus, children, what a rumpus!"

The swaggering, boisterous Courbet was one of the great egocentrics in the history of painting. "I am a Courbetist, that's all," he declared; "my painting is the only true one; I am the foremost and the sole artist of this century." One may assume that he came very early to regard it as normal for him to occupy the center of the stage, for he was the only male among the five children of a family of well-to-do peasants. Gustave was born at Ornans, a small village in eastern France near Besançon, on June 10, 1819. His father wanted him to become an engineer and imposed on him the stiff scholastic load that this calling required. Unfortunately, the boy's tastes were diametrically opposed to this program. Hiking, fishing, hunting, swimming were his fortes. His passion was nature and with it came a natural inclination to draw. After a decade of school, which he was later to recall as "years of forced labor," Courbet at last convinced his father to let him give up his scientific career and allow him to study law in Paris.

For Courbet, as for many other young men of the time who wanted to get off on their own, the law was a convenient pretext—to be quickly dropped. He arrived in Paris in 1840 and lost little time in devoting himself entirely to painting. But no more forced labor, no more school for him. The only academy frequented by the young Courbet was the

Seated at his easel, painting a landscape, Courbet displays what he proudly called his "Assyrian profile" in this detail from his huge canvas *The Painter's Studio (page 51)*. The painting is realistic in detail—the nude is based on a photograph—but allegorical in content. The small boy may represent innocence or the future; the nude is perhaps the artist's muse or Nature herself.

Courbet: *The Painter's Studio* (detail), 1855

Atelier Suisse where, for a modest fee, anyone could study living models. (Among others who later studied there were Monet and Cézanne.) "I never had a master, never!" Courbet was to boast: "I am the pupil of nature." This was, as usual, an exaggeration. Seldom had the Louvre seen a more assiduous visitor. Titian, Rembrandt and Velázquez—he soaked up the great masters with the same gargantuan appetite with which he downed his tankards of beer.

And soon it was in Paris as it had been at Ornans: he stole the show. At the Andler Keller, one of the first Parisian *brasseries*—or beer halls—teeming with journalists, medical students, printmakers and billiard players, Courbet became the center of a noisy group of writers and artists, holding forth, puffing on his pipe, guffawing or singing folk ballads of his own invention. Strikingly handsome—he was described as an Assyrian with doe's eyes—as long as poverty kept his figure trim, he was at once profoundly ingratiating and irritating, conceited and sincere, an exhibitionist, but warmly generous. His good humor and self-confidence were contagious. Friends thronged to the huge studio where he camped (rather than lived) and where he painted amidst visitors who argued, recited verse, sang or read in a corner. He had the naïveté but also the immense vigor of a peasant. He clung to his provincial Jura accent, continued to sport the white waistcoat that he had cut from one of his grandmother's petticoats, and he kept his money in a sock.

His loyalty to his origins paid off. It was the peasants of Ornans who projected him with startling suddenness to the forefront of French painting. He had been trying his hand, none too successfully, at literary subjects and, with far better results, at romantic portraits of his sisters and, of course, of himself. Gradually, however, the romantic haze lifted, and he began to devote his attention to the people he knew, the stiff-jointed, homely folk of Ornans.

P easants were not newcomers to canvas; they were one of the favorite subjects of genre, a form of painting that dealt with popular scenes, often in a droll, somewhat condescending manner, perfected by the Flemish and Dutch painters of the 17th Century. These genre paintings were extremely popular in mid-19th Century France, but they were diminutive in size and scope. Courbet painted his country people life-sized. This change in scale made all the difference; by lending them the heroic dimensions until then reserved for historical painting, Courbet literally raised the road workers and farmers of his hometown to the dignity of history. They are shown as they are, their faces furrowed and their minds blunted by a lifetime of labor, their hands gnarled and their feet heavy with mud; there is nothing sentimental or idealized about them. The swarthy *Stone Breakers* and the careworn mourners of the huge *Burial at Ornans (pages 50-51)* that Courbet exhibited at the Salon in 1850 marked the victory of real, contemporary people over mythological and religious figures. *Burial at Ornans*, Courbet rightly bragged, was "the burial of Romanticism."

It was all so natural for Courbet. He painted the segment of life that he knew best, the people and the landscapes of Ornans. Art, he professed, "is a wholly physical language whose words are all the visible

In the 1850s, the Andler Keller *brasserie* —shown here in a rare etching by Courbet—was a noisy eating and drinking spot favored by many leading French artists and writers. It was only two doors away from Courbet's studio, and he could be found there virtually every day arguing his revolutionary ideas about realism in art. "The *brasserie* was merely an extension of his studio," wrote a critic, Jules-Antoine Castagnary. "It was at the *brasserie* that he established contact with the outside world."

objects." Angels cannot be depicted, because they cannot be seen. The role of the artist is not to create but to see what exists. "To paint a bit of country, one must know it," he said. "Me, I know my country. Those woods, that's our home; that river is the Loue. Go see them and you will see my picture." Or, as he wrote on another occasion, painting "can only consist in the representation of objects visible and tangible to the artist." This simple doctrine was the subject of interminable discussions, as confused as they were heated, among Courbet's friends at the Andler Keller and at the Brasserie des Martyrs, until the day when somebody (probably the novelist and art critic Champfleury) condensed them into a magical catchword: Realism.

Realism, as championed by Courbet, was perfectly in keeping with the spirit of the times. The rise of the bourgeoisie marked the victory of material concerns, material progress, material values. Courbet would have agreed wholeheartedly with Auguste Comte, whose philosophy of positivism permeated the thinking of the day: "All real knowledge rests on facts." Like Courbet, experimental medicine, just then in the process of being defined by the physiologist Claude Bernard, rejected the abstract in favor of the concrete. Its purpose was, as Bernard wrote, "to obtain exact facts by means of rigorous observation." Furthermore, the weight and solidity, the sheer physical density of content and form in Courbet's work would seem to have reflected perfectly the down-to-earth aspirations of the middle class.

But indignation, not admiration, was their response. Over the years, at least 20 of Courbet's canvases were to be rejected by the jury of the Salon. "Great God! How ugly!" exclaimed a journalist when he saw the *Burial at Ornans*. Public opinion agreed. When Napoleon III visited the Salon of 1853, he expressed his disgust with the monumental *Bathers* by lashing the girl's rump with his riding crop. A more polite visitor, the critic Delécluze, limited himself to a verbal whipping. "His bather is so monstrously ugly," he wrote, "that she would spoil a crocodile's appetite." When Courbet, 17 years after the *Burial*, arranged a retrospective exhibit of his work, two of the most perceptive critics of the time, the brothers Jules and Edmond de Goncourt, merely echoed the prevailing opinion: "Nothing, nothing, and nothing in this show of Courbet's . . . the ugly then, always the ugly. . . ."

And how, asked his well-to-do audience, could he expect to produce anything but ugliness, considering his subject matter, the lower classes? Ugliness was their distinguishing feature, as beauty was that of the upper classes. Courbet's, clearly, was an art of the people, for the people and by the people; and as such, it could only be distasteful to good society. It was, in the words of Count de Nieuwerkerke, Napoleon III's Superintendent of Fine Arts, "an art for democrats." The objection to Courbet was as much social and political as it was esthetic.

He did nothing to dispel the confusion between politics and esthetics —on the contrary. "Realism," he affirmed, "is by essence the art of democracy." Permeated by the vague, idealistic brand of socialism current on the eve of the revolution of 1848, he had sided with the popular insurrection. The same year the Salon, in the democratic spirit of the day, was thrown open without restriction to all comers. In this wide-open, juryless Salon of 1848 he exhibited 10 works. "Were it not for the February Revolution," he later wrote, "possibly no one would ever have seen my paintings." He remained loyal to the spirit of '48— provocatively so. He flaunted his popular sympathies, accentuated his peasant manners and gleefully spat his contempt for state and church in the face of the bourgeoisie. "Gustave Courbet, master painter, without ideal and without religion," proclaimed his letterhead.

Needless to say, socialists made the most of this prestigious convert to their cause. "Formerly art was made for gods and princes. Perhaps the time has come to make art for man," preached art critic Théophile Thoré-Bürger; another critic, Jules-Antoine Castagnary, hailed Courbet as "a Velázquez of the people." The radical theoretician Pierre-Joseph Proudhon regarded *The Stone Breakers* as the first socialist picture ever painted. Proudhon and Courbet became close friends. The artist painted a powerful portrait of the writer. The latter wrote a verbose, art-blind book in which he presented Courbet as the father of a doctrine that, some 60 years later, was—with disastrous effects—to become the official dogma in Soviet Russia: socialist realism.

Yet Courbet the artist was not as revolutionary as Courbet the man. True, his aim was "to translate the customs, ideas, aspects of my time . . . in a word, to produce living art," but the idiom he used was firmly entrenched in the past. Again and again he declared that the way for an individual to express himself fully was to carry on a personal study of tradition. The difference between himself and the academic artists whom he despised lay precisely in the fact that they were too weak to carry this investigation far enough. Yet this was a difference in degree, not in kind. "I traversed tradition as a good swimmer would cross a river; the academicians drown in it." Pictorially, Courbet's popular scenes held their own with the masters consecrated by the museum. He might be dubbed a Velázquez of the people, or as another critic put it "the Raphael of paving stones"; the fact remained that he *was* of the same race of titans as Raphael and Velázquez. Even a hostile critic like Paul de Saint-Victor admitted it: "He paints solid things solidly; his technique is that of the masters."

Such a man was reclaimable. If only he would renounce his objectionable subject matter, his sins might easily be forgiven. Courbet was never irretrievably banned from the Salon. Even during his most embattled years, paintings whose themes were not thought objectionable won acceptance and sometimes applause. And when, in the 1860s, he increasingly turned from polemical works burdened with political overtones to the depiction of landscapes, still lifes and hunting scenes, the officialdom of the Second Empire was willing to open its arms to the repentant prodigal son. Did not the government of Napoleon III offer to decorate him with the Legion of Honor?

But Courbet turned it down. His convictions were unchanged. When the Second Empire collapsed in 1870 he applauded and enthusiastically welcomed the government of the socialist Commune of Paris that followed. In it he saw a reincarnation of the Republic of 1848. The insurrectional government put him in charge of artistic affairs and, in this office, he played a role in the tearing down of one of the city's detested symbols of Napoleonism, the column in the Place Vendôme.

The following year the conservative government of Versailles ruthlessly crushed the Commune. Courbet, a broken man, was dragged into court and, after several months in prison, was sentenced to pay the cost of re-erecting the Vendôme column. Insulted, persecuted, he fled to Switzerland in 1873 and settled at La Tour-de-Peilz, on Lake Geneva.

For Courbet, exile was disastrous. It brought the one thing that could really hurt him: neglect, oblivion. No more rumpus about him. For conservative society, he was now beyond consideration. His pictures were refused at the Salon of 1872; about one of them, his colleague Ernest Meissonier, an esteemed historical painter, said, "We need not look at it. It is not a question of art but of dignity; Courbet cannot appear at our exhibitions. He must be considered dead as far as we are concerned." Worse, Courbet had ceased to interest the younger generation of artists—Manet and the circle of painters beginning to cluster around him. For the bourgeoisie, he was too progressive; for the new avantgarde, he had been outstripped by progress. Suffering from dropsy, he became bloated to monstrous proportions, until at last he could no longer rise. Looking at the lake, he sighed: "If only I could swim in it, were it only five minutes, I would be cured!" He died December 31, 1877.

The political objections of the bourgeoisie and the artistic objections of the avant-garde brought Courbet's art a disrepute from which it has not completely recovered to this day. Opposite and dissimilar as they were, the criticisms of the two groups were related in that they both took issue with Courbet's subject matter. The bourgeoisie disliked his choice of subjects; the artists disliked the fact that he emphasized subject so much. And indeed, there is no doubt that Courbet believed in the fundamental Renaissance postulate that it was the subject that made the work. For him, painting was still a mirror.

What made him superior to other painters, in his view, was not that he transformed reality into something new, but simply that he saw reality more sharply. Once he was painting a landscape outdoors, in the company of a friend. "What is that?" he asked his companion, pointing to a grayish mass in the distance. Then he looked down at his canvas and added: "Oh, it's faggots." His picture's eyesight was, one might say, sharper than his own—so sharp and precise was it, in fact, that he

On a festive May afternoon in 1871, as a patriotic crowd cheered in the Place Vendôme in Paris and a band played the *Marseillaise*, a tall column topped with a statue of Napoleon came crashing down (*above*). The Vendôme Column had been built as a monument to French valor, but the radical Communards who governed Paris briefly after the War of 1870 saw it as a shrine to the hated Bonapartes and ordered its destruction. Among the group inspecting the toppled statue in the photograph below is Courbet (the heavy, bearded figure in the middle of the second row), who was head of the Paris Commune Art Commission.

once boasted of a set of pictures, "They are as exact as mathematics."

Yet despite his aggressive fidelity to subject matter and to reality, a subtle change had infected Courbet's work that went undetected by public and artists alike. It was a change that upset the very postulate Courbet honored—that painting was a language placed at the disposal of subject matter—and it never occurred to Courbet that he was questioning it. He was a great talker, and he wanted his pictures to be like him, to deliver a message; but when he painted, the garrulous Courbet was irresistibly attracted to silence. The figures in some of his finest works are asleep: *The Sleeping Spinner*, whose color is tempered as one quiets one's voice in order not to wake a sleeper; *The Sleeping Blonde*, who seems caught in the lull between the distant beats of a heart slowed down by deep slumber; the sensuously entangled women of *Sleep*, and a half dozen more. And the dark, monumental frieze of *Burial at Ornans* —Courbet's artistic manifesto and masterpiece—is concerned with the deepest sleep of all, death.

Courbet's huge work *The Painter's Studio (pages 36 and 51)* is shadowed by the same silence, even though it was designed to deliver a specific message. Courbet subtitled it "a real allegory summarizing seven years of my artistic life," and every figure in it meant something. The artist sitting at his easel, a female nude, a little boy symbolize the forces of life. On the right are all those "who live off life": his friends, such as Champfleury and Baudelaire, as well as collectors; on the left are gathered all those "who live off death": priest, undertaker's assistant, merchant, war veteran. At least, Courbet meant them to mean something; actually the viewer is less aware of their standing *for* something than of their just standing *about*. What binds them is not a literary meaning but a kind of passive resistance against the obligation to signify anything other than their own presence. Their resistance appears to have been quite successful, for even Courbet found his allegory "passably obscure." For the first time, a picture using rhetorical devices falls prey to stillness. The message, the talk, are blurred, hushed, as if they had been swallowed up by the muteness of the huge, vibrantly modulated wall that closes and dominates the canvas.

This fascination with silence explains Courbet's interest in peasants. Unlike his contemporary, Jean-François Millet, who sentimentalized rural life and forced his sowers, reapers and shepherdesses to carry, in addition to their crushing load of labor, the burden of a moral and social message, Courbet cherishes them for this distrust of, and resistance to, words. Silence restores the kinship between man and the realm of nature. Mystery is infused by the intense stillness of Courbet's models— not the psychological enigma of a Mona Lisa, but the mystery of sheer physical presence. The depth of a smile or a glance lies outside of Courbet's world. He knows only the depth of a spring, of a forest.

In the middle of *The Painter's Studio*, Courbet has placed what matters most to him, a landscape. For earth is the prime depository and source of nature's inexhaustible and indivisible energy. To Courbet all physical things are different manifestations of the same power of life, and he depicts them with the same majestic breadth. His landscapes are saturated with a feeling of feminine fecundity, and his women are as ample as landscapes. In the monumental *Young Women on the Banks of the Seine (pages 52-53)* two young ladies lying on a riverbank are seen in the languid, dreamy, semi-vacant state that precedes sleep. They are weighed down by somnolence, as if about to be absorbed by the soil. But the downward pressure of the girls' bodies is contradicted by the slow, formidable upward surge of the earth. They seem but larger petals amidst the flowers in the grass, burgeonings on the surface of nature that present inconsistent appearances if viewed in themselves, but that are dense with life's density. This silent density fills the picture to the brim and presents us with a solid, impenetrable front.

Indeed the solid, silent front of the earth is Courbet's fundamental vision: no motif occurs more frequently in his landscapes than the cliff. Even the ocean's waves—in what he rightly calls his "sea landscapes" *(page 54)*—rear up with massive, clifflike stability. Perspectives and forms tilt forward, as if erected by the energy within them, and press themselves against that untransgressible limit, the picture plane.

Thus, quite involuntarily, Courbet has come right to the brink of the 19th Century's major artistic revolution: the reduction of painting to its own surface, which no longer functions as a mirror or a window opened on the world. Lines and colors cease to express objects; they are no longer transparent means but opaque ends. By the most startling of paradoxes, the painter most eager to express the reality of things and creatures is confronted, on his canvas, with the reality of paint—its autonomous thickness and shapes. The freedom of Courbet's hand in applying color to canvas has seldom been equaled. He heaps up the pigments with brush or palette knife so lustily that he appears to have forgotten his initial aim of representing a figure or a landscape. In truth, the reality of things, or images, has been contradicted by the reality of paint, or texture.

What saved Courbet from being confused by the dilemma posed by the fundamental opposition of paint and image—which has been puzzling painters ever since—is the fact that he never became aware of it. His naïveté and self-confidence saved him. He "produced paintings as an apple-tree produces apples," said a friend. What could possibly go wrong when a natural painter paints nature? Confusions between texture and image, between paint and subject are accidents that befall common mortals, not a Courbet, who can boast: "I paint like God."

That explains why, despite his apparent qualifications for the part, Gustave Courbet was not the first scandalous painter. To be scandalous, one must be aware of the strangeness of one's behavior. Manet was aware of, and upset by, the conflict between the act of painting and what is painted; Courbet was not. How could he be worried by the ambiguities and contradictions implicit in his work, since he did not see them? Compare those two historic canvases, related in so many ways, *Young Women on the Banks of the Seine* and *Luncheon on the Grass,* and the difference becomes glaringly evident: the former was painted, so to speak, before the fall, i.e., before consciousness of the great dilemma; the latter was painted after.

"A Democratic Art"

First among the artistic revolutions that erupted in mid-19th Century art was that of the Realists, who vehemently rejected the subject matter of the then popular schools of painting, Neoclassicism and Romanticism. Fed up with what one critic identified as "Greek visions, Roman visions, medieval visions, visions of the 16th, 17th and 18th Centuries," the Realists painted the world around them. Some of them went so far as to straightforwardly portray the lower classes, people usually considered too ordinary to serve as fitting subjects for fine art.

At the forefront of the Realist movement was the brash and controversial Gustave Courbet, whose 1849 painting, *The Stone Breakers,* can be said to have started the trend toward down-to-earth themes. An articulate theorist, Courbet called for a "negation of the ideal" and the creation of "a democratic art." Less outspoken was Camille Corot, who was possessed by an almost reverential love of nature. In such modest landscapes as the one opposite, Corot defied the prevailing fashion that scorned such mundane, unromantic scenes. Honoré Daumier and Jean-François Millet concentrated on peasants, workers and the everyday look of the city and countryside.

By 1866, with Courbet's belated success at the Salon, the Realists' revolution of subject matter was complete. On its foundation, Manet and the Impressionists had already begun to carry out a new and startling revolution of technique to record contemporary life.

When he created this misty view of the town of Mantes seen through a screen of shimmering trees, Corot was drawing upon nearly 50 years of experience in painting landscapes. Earlier, when such a picture was exhibited at the Salon of 1849, carping academic critics insisted upon calling it a "study," for it lacked the "finish" they demanded. Corot's landscapes eventually won him a large, enthusiastic audience.

Camille Corot: *The Cathedral at Mantes,* 1865-1869

Jean-François Millet: *The Washerwoman*, c.1861

Jean-François Millet spent most of his life in Barbizon near Paris painting peasants like the ones he had known while growing up in Normandy. A sentimental man, he felt a strong nostalgia for the pre-industrial past, and his pictures evoke what he called the "homely goodness" of countryfolk whose struggle to survive lends them nobility. Millet's *Washerwoman (above)* is almost stately, posed in front of a roaring fire like a heroine of toil: critics called Millet the "Michelangelo of the peasants."

Less sentimental than Millet was Daumier, who

Honoré Daumier: *The Washerwoman*, c.1863

believed that "one must be of one's time." His place was Paris, where he had lived since boyhood, and where, from his studio at 9 Quai d'Anjou, he might have observed the washerwoman above, gently assisting her child up the steep Seine bank. Silhouetted against the bright façade of buildings across the river, mother and child exist in a veil of shadow that recalls the chiaroscuro of Rembrandt, whom Daumier admired. Rising monumentally from the foreground, they suggest that Daumier, more than Millet, should be likened to Michelangelo.

Gustave Courbet was born in Ornans, near the Swiss border of France. Fittingly, his most controversial early paintings are set in Ornans and peopled with its inhabitants. Perhaps inspired by the death of his grandfather—whose advice to the young artist was, "Shout loudly and march straight ahead"—Courbet created a huge, friezelike burial scene, including some 40 life-sized portraits: Curé Bonnet, the parish priest, is reading prayers; corpulent Mayor Prosper Teste de Sagey stands next to the grave; gravedigger Cassard kneels beside the open pit. At the far right are Courbet's mother and three sisters; at the far left, behind the pallbearers is Grandfather Oudot, his likeness adapted from an earlier portrait. Far from winning the success he expected of it, the picture—although shown at the Salon of 1850-1851—was attacked by critics, who were shocked by the artist's depiction of so commonplace and depressing an event on a scale usually reserved for grand, uplifting subjects.

A similar fate befell Courbet's *The Painter's Studio (opposite)*, which was refused at the Exposition Universelle of 1855. An immensely complex work, it represents the arts at the right, personified by Courbet's friends and mentors; at the left are realistically represented but symbolic figures of the poor with their exploiters. Courbet's mixture of reality, allegory, social comment and portraiture mystified his viewers.

Gustave Courbet: *The Painter's Studio, A Real Allegory Summarizing a Period of Seven Years of My Artistic Life*, 1855

Gustave Courbet: *The Burial at Ornans*, 1849

The volatile Courbet evidently took his grandfather's advice to heart after being notified that only 11 of the 14 paintings he submitted to the Exposition Universelle of 1855 had been accepted. Particularly outraged at the jury's rejection of his *Painter's Studio* and *Burial at Ornans*, Courbet decided to erect his own gallery on the fairgrounds. But after the initial excitement generated by his rebelliousness died down, Courbet's exhibit was attended by only a thin trickle of visitors, and the project ended as a financial loss. One of those who came, however, was the great Delacroix, who wrote of the *Painter's Studio* in his journal: "I simply could not tear myself away from it . . . . They have refused one of the most singular paintings of our time; but a strapping lad like Courbet is not going to be discouraged by so small a thing as that."

Indeed, within two years after his failure at the Exposition Universelle, Courbet began to find regular acceptance at the official Salons. Yet a breath of scandal still hung over the controversial painter. While praising Courbet's technical achievement, critic Théophile Gautier wrote that *Young Women on the Banks of the Seine (right)* belonged "in that extravagant category to which the artist owes his notoriety . . . a deafening tattoo on the tom-tom of publicity to attract the attention of the unheeding mob." It is difficult today to find what Gautier found so objectionable in this seemingly innocuous view of two young ladies escaping the heat of mid-summer on a shaded river bank. Perhaps it was a certain coarseness in their features, a hint that they might not be proper *demoiselles*. Perhaps it was their very contemporaneity: it might be acceptable to show two nymphs or Roman maidens napping in the open air, but two Parisian shopgirls? Unthinkable! This same moral revulsion at contemporary (and, hence, vulgar) subjects would be aroused in the next decade by Manet's scandalous *Luncheon on the Grass* and *Olympia*, which offended even more by showing contemporary women nude.

After 1857, though, Courbet's work became less controversial. By 1866 he was the darling of the Salon. In 1870 he was offered the Legion of Honor. Characteristically, he refused, declaring, "I am 50 years old and I have always lived in freedom; let me end my life free. When I am dead, let it be said of me: 'He belonged to no school, to no church, to no institution, to no academy, least of all to any regime except the regime of liberty.' "

Gustave Courbet: *Young Women on the Banks of the Seine*, 1856

Gustave Courbet: *Waves,* 1869

Nature pure and simple became as much a subject for the Realists as people and everyday life. Corot and a group of artists who became known as the Barbizon School retreated to the forests for their settings; others chose the sea. With its varying moods, its swift changes of light and color, the sea was a natural choice.

Courbet, who also did a number of forest scenes, painted seascapes with a particular emphasis on the drama of waves. Following what was then general practice, Courbet made sketches from nature; essentially, however, he composed and finished his pictures in the studio. As the Realist painters became more interested in capturing a specific moment, they began to abandon studio work and paint directly from nature, so-called plein-air painting. The vivid watercolor at the upper right was created by Johan-Barthold Jongkind, a Dutchman living in France, as he stood on the beach at St. Adresse, on the Normandy coast. In the traditional manner, however, he continued to paint his formal landscapes indoors.

One of the first true plein-air painters was Eugène Boudin, the owner of a frame shop in Le Havre. A mentor of the young Claude Monet, Boudin scrupulously labeled his pastels and watercolors of the seaside with the date, time of day and even the speed and direction of the wind, noting in his sketchbook that "everything that is painted on the spot has a strength, a power, a vividness of touch that one does not find again in the studio." It was his insistence on these primary impressions on the artist and his use of the leisured middle class as subjects worthy of attention, that made Boudin a powerful influence on the Impressionists who followed.

Johan-Barthold Jongkind: *Beach at St. Adresse*, 1863

Eugène Boudin: *Beach at Trouville*, 1864

III

Painter of
the Present

If Manet believed that the uproar about *Luncheon on the Grass* had been
an accident, he was soon to be set straight. *Luncheon*'s reception was
mild compared to the insults, sarcasms and indignation unleashed by
Manet's contribution to the Salon of 1865. It ranked, and still ranks, as
one of the greatest scandals in art history. "The Exhibition has its buf-
foon," wrote Judith Gautier. Her father, Théophile Gautier, agreed:
"Monsieur [Manet] has the honor of being a danger. But the danger is
over now." The public smothered the aggressor under derision. "An ep-
idemic of wild laughter prevails," a review reported, "in front of the
canvases by Manet."

There were two Manet works in the Salon, but the one that caused
the most trouble was *Olympia (pages 70-71)*. "The crowd gathers before *Olympia* as at the morgue," gloated the critic Paul de Saint-Victor.
He and his colleagues subjected the young girl, resting naked on a bed
while a Negro maid presents her with a bouquet, to a verbal lynching.
"Harlot," "female gorilla," "the ultimate in ugliness," "vulgar virgin,"
"yellow-bellied odalisque" were some of the epithets applied to the pale
damsel. "Women on the point of giving birth and proper young girls
would be well advised to flee this spectacle," one reviewer admonished.
But his warning went unheeded. So huge and boisterous grew the
crowds mobbing *Olympia* that two guards were stationed in front of it.
In fact, a few days after the opening of the Salon the controversial canvas was removed to the highest reaches on the most remote wall of the
exhibition hall.

It took *Olympia* more than 40 years to live down the shame. Offered
by public subscription to France in 1890 at the instigation of a group of
Manet's admirers headed by Claude Monet, it was hung in the Musée
du Luxembourg until 1907, when Prime Minister Georges Clemenceau,
who once posed for Manet, ordered that it be moved to the more prestigious showcase of the Louvre. "Take care nobody sees you!" the
official from the Ministry told the curator in charge of the operation.
And, in fact, the picture was transferred as unobtrusively as a danger-
ous political prisoner—in a horse-cab at eight in the morning.

Today it is still possible to sense what so shocked public and critics a century ago. Everywhere in *Olympia* the will to simplify is obvious. The picture is built on brutal contrasts. The light foreground is pitted against the dark-brown and dark-green rectangles of the background. It makes use again of the oppositions of dressed versus naked, black versus white figures already used in *Luncheon on the Grass*. The simplicity and bluntness of Manet's ingredients related his paintings, in his contemporaries' eyes, less to the refined art of painting than to the pictures on playing cards, or to the popular *images d'Épinal*, crudely colored cartoonlike reproductions of popular subjects turned out in the town of Épinal in eastern France. Courbet called *Olympia* "the Queen of Spades . . . after her bath," and another critic spoke of "an almost childlike ignorance of the rudiments of draftsmanship, an inconceivable determination to be vulgar."

Would a real painter have made himself guilty of the cluster of smears composing the bouquet of flowers or of the loose trails of grayish paint signifying the folds of the bed sheets? No, for he would have known that to give the impression of being a faithful mirror, a painting must be smooth. To impose the illusion of being a window on the world, the painter must try to hide, as best as possible, the means used to achieve that illusion. Transitions are rendered imperceptible by means of modeling, carefully graded shading, polished brushwork.

Manet does nothing to hide the painter's hand; he even underscores its intervention with a thick, blackish outline that encompasses the figure of Olympia. Traditionalists regarded Manet with the same annoyance magicians feel for a colleague who shows the audience how a trick is done. Manet's visible brushwork and emphasis on flat surface patterns deny deception by never allowing us to forget that what we see is merely pigment on a piece of canvas. The painter's reality, Manet tells us, is much more than the people and places he sees about him—it is, first and foremost, paint.

This does not mean that he turns his back on life. Quite the contrary. Even the most agile realist, like Courbet, lags behind the contemporary world that he seeks to render. Manet is eager to seize the immediate. Throughout the late 1850s and early 1860s he had been moving toward the conviction that, for the artist, the only actual moment is the moment when he paints. This was a new, absolute kind of realism: Courbet painted the present; Manet painted *in* the present. In *Olympia*, this revolutionary procedure ceased to hide behind Spanish precedents. What impressed people, what shocked them, was the girl's nakedness; but they wrongly ascribed it to her shamelessness—the nakedness proclaimed by Manet was that of paint.

Manet's critics felt, albeit they did not fathom, this unheard of nudity. "Patches," "flat areas," "cut-outs" are among the most common reproaches hurled against his painting. More benevolently disposed critics, like Castagnary, agreed: "Manet possesses to the highest point the feeling for the colorful blotch." Now, blotches are surface occurrences. All painting, to be sure, is basically an operation performed on the two-dimensional canvas. Until Manet, however, artists had sought to disguise its two-dimensionality and to persuade us, by means of such devices as perspective, modeling and shadowing, that viewers had access to that essential platform on which the world of reality rests, the third dimension. Manet prevents the spectator's eye from plunging into make-believe depth; instead, he forces us to dwell on the surface of the picture. Thus, the artist forces the viewer to see Olympia not only as a naked girl, but also as patches of paint laid on the surface of the canvas. Such simplification and heightening of line in *The Street Singer* caused a critic to describe the woman's eyebrows as "commas"; in *The Luncheon (pages 76-77)*, the lemon on the table may have been part of the meal but more importantly it answers Manet's need for a spot of yellow.

This bold, surface-hugging way of applying paint makes Manet's pictures strike out at us instead of receding into fictional perspective space. In so doing, they undercut the very foundations on which painting had rested since the time of Giotto, Dürer and Leonardo da Vinci. The space that these artists explored and filled with the fruits of their observations, beliefs or imagination was staked out by the lines of perspective, which start at all points of the picture plane and converge to a hypothetical point in the imaginary background of the painting. The unusual, sometimes apparently awkward characteristics of Manet's work during the period between 1860 and 1870 may all be traced to the effects of a revolution—the destruction of three-dimensional perspective—of which the premonitory rumblings could have been heard in the work of Ingres, Delacroix and, above all, Courbet. The paintings of Manet's early Spanish period had been original, but only indirectly so. The next period, ushered in by *Luncheon on the Grass* in 1863, is one of masterful statements, at times direct to the point of brutality. Varied as these pictures are—portraits, still lifes, seascapes, historical and genre paintings—they tell, when put together, a coherent story: the decline and death of perspective.

The coherence, however, is not strictly chronological. Often a more advanced picture precedes a more conservative one, as if Manet were trying to apologize for his own—sometimes involuntary—excesses. Perhaps he disobeyed the laws of perspective as reluctantly as he had revolted against the proscriptions of his father or of the École. But he could not help it. His intense feeling for the surging immediacy of life drove him to seek, in his painting, effects of a similar immediacy, which were incompatible with the recessive nature of perspective. His lines refuse to recede toward the vanishing point where the visible turns into the imaginary. Under his brush, planes that are meant to lead the eye to a distant horizon sometimes turn instead into parallel strips, so that the effect is not one of horizontal recession but of vertical accumulation.

When the road into the illusion of the third dimension is thus barricaded, the viewer's eye is brought abruptly to a halt. In *The Execution of the Emperor Maximilian (page 72)*, a wall cuts off all but a narrow glimpse of landscape; the protagonists of Manet's first and last important pictures, *The Absinthe Drinker* and *A Bar at the Folies-Bergère*, have their backs to a wall. Indeed, even when he sought to open up a wide ex-

The three toreadors in Manet's *Bullfight (above)* were originally mere background observers in a larger canvas called *Incident in the Bullring.* But this picture aroused such violent critical attacks that Manet sliced it up, salvaging the upper portion as *Bullfight* and the lower part as *The Dead Toreador (pages 32-33).* The contemporary cartoon below gives a rough idea of what the original looked like. It bore the caption, "Having had reason to complain about his paint merchant, Mr. Manet resolves henceforth to use only his inkwell," a reference to Manet's deep blacks. Another critic, commenting on the undramatic relationship between the toreador and the bull, wrote: "Upon awakening, a bullfighter sees a bull six miles away; unmoved, he turns over and heroically goes back to sleep."

panse of territory, the result looked wall-like. Of *The Battle of the Kearsarge and the Alabama (page 73),* which depicts a naval engagement off Cherbourg in which the Confederate vessel *Alabama* was sunk by a Yankee man-of-war, a satirist wrote that the battle apparently took place on "a vertical slice of the ocean." The sympathetic Castagnary found this seascape "a bit like a façade but very straightforward," and was obviously unaware that it was precisely the straightforwardness that caused the wall-like effect: by laying on his pigments in frank, sharp contrasts, Manet excluded those subtle gradations of tones that are perspective's fifth column within the ranks of color and form.

Manet noticed the drying-up of space's depth, the reduction to the picture plane that marks the real beginning of modern painting, and was aware that the progressive closing of the gap between background and picture plane created a set of terribly difficult new problems for the execution of a successful painting. Trapped in the narrowing gap, the figures of Manet's pictures became flattened, disoriented, as in the strange, masterful *Balcony (page 76).* Between the shrill, geometric pattern of the railing (coinciding, like a collage, with the surface) and the dark-gray, compact background, the foreground's threesome looks less like a social gathering than like a trio of captives packed in a green-barred cell too small for them. *The Balcony* is puzzling in several ways. Despite their closeness, the scene's occupants seem utterly unrelated—a fact underscored by the diverging directions of their stares. In addition, the figures are inexpressive. The face of the woman on the right says no more than the huge flower on her head; the man's features are less important than his preposterously blue necktie. This muteness, this refusal of human figures to be meaningful was one of the problems that scandalized Manet's time—and still sometimes troubles ours. But it does tell with masterful conciseness a different kind of dramatic story: the story of what happens to painting when space dries up. The work of Manet during the 1860s boldly explores every implication, every episode of this drama.

Not only were figures to suffer from the shrinking of space. It is easy to picture action on a stage constructed by perspective's lines. When they disappear, action tends to freeze, leaving the painter little choice but to represent immobile subjects. Station is emphasized at the expense of action. In *The Battle of the Kearsarge and the Alabama,* the stirring naval engagement is removed to the horizon, leaving a sea practically empty except for a harmless sailboat. Psychological depth, too, suffers from the loss of the recesses opened up by perspective. On the surface to which Manet was mercilessly reducing painting, emotion finds no more room than motion. His figures are uninvolved, uncommunicative. Discussing Manet's *Portrait of Émile Zola (page 69)* the painter Odilon Redon wrote, "It is rather a still life, so to speak, than the expression of a human being."

Indeed, Manet was very quickly accepted as a painter of still lifes—nobody expected oysters or apples to talk. But the Mr. Hyde in Manet was not content with this easy way out. He was driven to prove that the silence of paint was not due to the nature of his subject matter—and he made it quite clear by dealing with one of the most poignant events of his day in *The Execution of the Emperor Maximilian*. Maximilian, brave but foolish, had been urged in 1863 by Napoleon III to establish by force his claims as emperor of Mexico. However, political pressures (partly from the United States) caused Napoleon III to suspend military aid. The abandoned Maximilian was captured by the Mexicans, sentenced and shot to death. This tragedy shocked Frenchmen; they were horrified when they learned that it had caused Maximilian's young wife to go mad; and they blamed Napoleon III for its sinister outcome.

Horror, pity and resentment against Napoleon III prompted the republican Manet to picture the scene in no less than four canvases. Yet if one looks at them, one discovers practically no trace of the eloquent pathos that pervaded the masterpiece from which they derived their composition, Goya's *The Third of May, 1808*. They are cool, apparently detached works. The figure of the soldier loading his gun at the right attracts at least as much attention as the shooting on the left; and the artist appears less concerned with the death of Maximilian and his two companions than with the decorative uniforms of the riflemen. This strange attitude has caused Manet to be accused, to this day, of being indifferent, callous or—at best—as coldly objective as a reporter's camera. The opposite is true. Manet *was* deeply moved, and he made no deliberate attempt to stifle his emotion on canvas. But paint, when freed from the artifice of perspective, refuses to convey the message. *The Execution of the Emperor Maximilian* dramatically demonstrates the incompatibility of two-dimensional paint and storytelling. The silence of paint, it tells us, is stronger than the sight of blood and feeling of indignation. The real victim in *The Execution* is not Maximilian, but narrative.

There was one more step for Manet to take in his gradual, one might say reluctant, extermination of perspective. A gap still exists in *The Execution* between the picture plane and the wall before which the event takes place—a small gap, yet large enough to allow for some representation of the world. Once this gap closes, however, once the back wall coincides fully with the surface of the canvas, will it not be impossible to represent even a motionless image? Will the death of perspective not spell the death of any form of figuration? It was still too early in history to ask the question openly, but Manet clearly did sense the threat. He sought to stop, or at least to stall, the forward thrust of the background. In some pictures, the background falls back slightly, but such instances are mere reprieves. For them to be more, Manet would have had to forego the immediacy of the impact of paint that was his discovery. This, of course, he could not bring himself to do; and as a result, he was forced to face, again and again, the question: is it possible, considering the hold of tradition on our minds and eyes, to represent *any* subject matter without the help of the conventions of perspective?

In seeking a solution, Manet found encouragement in the Far East. In the background of his portrait of Zola, placed beside a photograph of *Olympia* and an etching by Goya after a painting by Velázquez, is a Japanese woodcut. In Japan the ancient popular medium of the woodcut had been raised to the dignity of great art at the turn of the 19th Century by two master printmakers, Utamaro and Hokusai. But Japan was not opened to the outside world until 1854, and only after that did Europeans become fully aware of its art. In 1856 a friend of Manet's, the engraver Félix Bracquemond, upon opening a parcel, found his attention attracted by the wrapping paper—it was a print from one of Hokusai's woodcut series. Bracquemond and, soon, others communicated their enthusiasm. Baudelaire wrote in 1861 that he had given his friends some of these Japanese *images d'Épinal* and that they "make a great effect."

To most people at the time the Japanese woodcuts were simply exotica. To Manet they brought proof that you could dispense with perspective and limit yourself to flat colors and lines and still do justice to subject matter—even to subject matter drawn from contemporary life. He studied these prints and learned from them—his friend Berthe Morisot said, "Only Manet and the Japanese are capable of indicating a mouth, eyes, a nose in a single stroke, but so concisely that the rest of the face takes on modeling." But, unlike many later admirers of Utamaro and Hokusai, Manet did not derive a recipe or a style from them. He sensed that the graphic art of the Japanese was so intimately involved with a culture in which word and image are closely connected that the art could not be transferred into the European context. Significantly, the only Manet works in which a direct influence is perceptible are his own drawings, etchings and lithographs—in particular his superb renditions of cats *(page 102)*. Japan gave him much needed encouragement; it did not provide him with a pat solution to the problem of shrinking space.

Manet was forced to work out his own, and he came up with an answer of the utmost daring: a flat figure silhouetted on a flat background. A striking illustration of the success of this solution is *The Fifer (page 56)*. It bursts upon us with all the exuberance that befits its youthful model. But, once again, Manet ran head on into public misunderstanding. One critic complained that the lone figure "is applied against a gray, monochrome background; no room, no air, no perspective; the poor fellow is pinned against an imaginary wall. . . . *The Fifer* is an amusing sample of a still barbarous imagery, a jack of diamonds nailed on a door."

Such criticism pained Manet, as it would throughout his life, and he did his utmost to hide his revolutionary artistic self behind a façade of politeness and frivolity. In 1866 a young writer who so far had written only romantic fiction and literary journalism, Émile Zola, turned art critic to plead the painter's cause. The following year, his acquaintance with the unrevolutionary side of Manet led him to write in a magazine article: "An artist's life, in our proper and orderly time, is that of a quiet bourgeois, who paints pictures in his studio as others sell pepper behind their counters."

But there were some people from whom Manet could not keep hidden the far from reassuring truth about his two-sided character: his models. All have testified to their awe when, in the secrecy of the stu-

Girl Rouging Her Lips, a woodblock print by the 18th Century master Utamaro, is representative of the Japanese art that delighted and influenced Manet and his contemporaries. Its subtle use of line, delicate color and flat perspective captivated the Impressionists, who at one time were themselves known as "the Japanese of painting." Claude Monet explained the special interest of his fellow painters when he praised that quality of Japanese art that "evokes presence by means of a shadow, the whole by means of a fragment."

dio, they saw Dr. Jekyll turn into Mr. Hyde. Manet painted in a kind of trance, one model recorded: "He was not always master of his hand, for he made use of no fixed technique and he had kept a schoolboy's frank naïveté before nature. In beginning a picture he could never have told how it would come out. If genius is made of unconsciousness and of the natural gift of truth, he certainly had genius." George Moore noted how "working under the immediate dictation of his eye, he snatched the tints instinctively, without premeditation." And when, some years later, Stéphane Mallarmé's turn to sit came, the poet was almost terrified to see the elegant member of café society turn into a savage in his studio and recorded "the frenzy with which he hurled himself at the empty canvas, blindly, as if he had never painted before."

Through these various testimonials, Manet's method becomes clear: it is the refusal of method. Memories, devices, routines are banished; only improvisation is allowed. He confided to a friend that every new painting was, for him, like throwing himself into the water without knowing how to swim. But in this deliberate ignorance lay the solution. To capture the present—a woman walking, a regatta—with the cumbersome, fastidious *métier* taught by the École—was like trying to time a 100-yard race with a cuckoo clock. Manet's revolutionary discovery was to realize that one could meet the presence of the subject only with the here-and-nowness of paint. The patient effort of analytic observation gave way to the instant flash of recognition. And he asked of the viewer of his picture the very same response that he demanded of himself vis-à-vis his model or subject: to experience it intuitively rather than to identify it.

The procedure was simple enough, but its very simplicity was what made it alien to eyes trained to view paintings only with the aid of complex Renaissance conventions. The reaction of Georges Clemenceau, a man of culture, to his portrait by Manet shows how easily misunderstandings could arise: "One of my eyes is missing," he said, "and my nose is crooked." On the other hand, the cook of Théodore Duret, Manet's friend, collector and biographer, reacted to her employer's portrait as the artist wanted everyone to: she said she was scared because she thought she was faced not with a picture but with a living person. Unfortunately, it was people of Clemenceau's training rather than the untutored cook whom Manet had to convince. To them, all he could say in self-justification was, "When it's there, it's there!"

And it wasn't always; his hit-or-miss, all-or-nothing approach made him fail more often than did less talented but more cautious artists. The only proof of sharing is the sharing itself. Hence his singular elation when he was given tangible evidence that such a sharing had occurred. In a letter, Manet recalls the grueling sessions for the portrait of Antonin Proust: "I remember, as if it were yesterday, the swift and summary fashion in which I treated the glove in the bare hand. And when at that moment you said to me: 'Please, not a stroke more,' I felt we were in such perfect agreement that I could not refrain from the pleasure of throwing my arms around you."

In 1867 Manet organized his own retrospective exhibition. He had several motives. The humiliations inflicted on him by the Salon jury impelled him to seek the public's verdict directly. Furthermore, a world's fair planned for 1867 by Napoleon III to extol the blessings lavished by his reign was going to bring to Paris art from every corner of the globe. Courbet, who had built a large pavilion to show his work in a similar exposition in 1855, chose to do so again. Manet decided to follow his example. In the unsigned preface to the catalogue of this show, which covered much of his work of the 1860s, he wrote: "Today the artist does not say 'Come see flawless works,' but 'Come see sincere works.'" And the preface added that he "has not attempted to overthrow ancient painting and to create a new one. He has simply tried to be himself and not somebody else."

As we have seen, the effect of Manet's revolution on the unprepared public was shattering. In turn, the public's reaction shattered Manet. "I wish I had you here," he had written in 1865 to his friend Baudelaire, then in Belgium. "Insults are pouring down on me as thick as hail." It was, if anything, an understatement. Critics, fellow painters, the public, even gossip columnists pounced on Manet. Baudelaire tried to comfort him, but was worried. "Manet has a strong talent, a talent which will resist," he confided to a mutual friend. "But he has a weak character. He seems to me disconsolate and dazed by the shock." Baudelaire's diagnosis was correct. Manet once wrote somewhat melodramatically to Antonin Proust, "The attacks of which I have been the object have broken the spring of life in me. . . . People don't realize what it feels like to be constantly insulted."

So, Manet took refuge in flight. In August 1865 he left for Spain. El Greco and Goya pleased him; Velázquez, his chief inspiration, ravished him and, no doubt, bolstered his shaken confidence. He was also glad to see in the flesh, in the *plaza del toros*, the bullfighters whom he had painted from imagination. But he got no farther than Madrid, defeated by Spanish food. The very smell of oil nauseated him. Once he almost quarreled with another Frenchman, sitting at the table next to him, because the latter devoured, with demonstrations of delight that the susceptible Manet attributed to mockery, the dishes that he himself refused to touch. Fortunately, the stranger was able to explain to Manet that he had just arrived from Portugal and that Spanish food seemed divine in comparison to Portuguese fare. He introduced himself: Théodore Duret, a cognac dealer. Soon he was to become the artist's staunch friend. After 10 days, Manet returned to France. When the passport controller at the border saw his name, he hastily called his wife and children to come gape at the famous M. Manet—they were surprised not to be confronted with an ogre.

"M. Manet studying the beauties of nature" is the caption of this cartoon from *Le Charivari*. It lampoons the artist's association with the Impressionists, who painted directly from nature, and ridicules Manet's penchant for picturing the women of cafés and concert halls rather than the sleek, idealized creatures of academic art. Such criticisms plagued Manet throughout his career. Even a year after his death, at a retrospective exhibition honoring him, a powerful critic called Manet's art "an enormous dung heap."

Many people were surprised. Manet was no latter-day Courbet: there was not a touch of bohemianism about him. He disapproved of swaggering, but he was very much the man-about-town, the dandy. Whenever he was not working, chances were you could see him strolling along the Boulevard, a short section of pavement near the Opéra that was like a concentrate of Parisian pleasures. Here were the fashionable restaurants and cafés: Tortoni, famous for its ice creams and its sidewalk tables graced by lavishly dressed *cocottes;* the Café Anglais, patronized by the social lions of the day; the Riche and the Bade where the intellectuals and celebrities convened. Manet had lunch at Tortoni's and the late afternoon invariably found him at the Bade, drinking apéritifs and smoking havanas in joyous, elegant company.

He cut a handsome figure on the Boulevard: dapper suits by the best tailors, a cane, pearl-gray top hat worn at an almost rakish angle, a carnation in his lapel; so impeccable was he, in fact, that George Moore felt there was something of the British gentleman about him. His appearance was not striking but very graceful *(pages 6 and 12).* Of medium height, he sported a golden beard and a halo of blond hair, whose gradual disappearance would have made him look older than he was had it not been for his sprightliness and boyish exuberance. His eyes were small, gray-blue and exceedingly mobile. In a word, he had charm.

And he was as nimble of wit as of limb. Delighting in conversation, skilled in the art of repartee, he shared the true Parisian's incapacity to refrain from the temptation of the *bon mot.* His cutting remarks were often repeated, as for instance his comment on Meissonier's laboriously realistic *The Charge of the Cuirassiers:* "Everything in this picture is metallic, except the armor plates." A commonplace historical painting by Jean-Paul Laurens, *The Death of Marceau,* representing the French revolutionary general surrounded by respectful Austrian colleagues, elicited the caustic comment: "These are cabdrivers mourning the death of the last stage coachman."

Manet not only possessed *esprit,* a French specialty, but also the Anglo-Saxon's humor, which is wit exerted at one's own expense. The Salon of 1876—where Manet's submissions had once again been refused—opened under a violent rainstorm; visitors reluctant to face the downpour remained inside, cluttering the exit and causing Manet, who had come, despite the jury's affront, to quip: "It goes to prove that it is as difficult to get out of the Salon as to get into it." He used his flawless manners to elude personal distress or irritation with a verbal pirouette. One of the critics most hostile to him for years was the German-born Albert Wolff, a figure so ugly and apelike the vitriolic Degas said of him that "he had come from Germany by way of the trees." Relenting at last, Wolff, toward the end of Manet's life, wrote some grudging compliments to the artist, who wrote back: "I thank you for the kind things you said about me, but I would not be displeased to read at last, while I am still alive, the wonderful article you will devote to me after my death."

Manet's verbal thrusts did not stem from a nasty character. On the contrary, he was modest, warm-hearted and he loved company—particularly the company of women. One of his deepest relationships was with Berthe Morisot, whose family belonged to the same upper-middle-class circle as Manet's. The two families knew each other, and it was natural that the talented Berthe, who had chosen to dedicate herself to painting and who had received lessons from Corot, should ask for Édouard's advice. She soon became his disciple. He was fascinated by her

When Manet married his former piano teacher Suzanne Leenhoff *(above)* in 1863, one of the guests at the wedding party was 11-year-old Léon Koëlla *(below)*. It is likely that Léon, who was born soon after Suzanne became Manet's mistress, was their son; but to avoid scandal, they always referred to him as Suzanne's younger brother. Manet became the boy's godfather.

proud, shy beauty, and at his request she posed for him—in the presence of a chaperone, of course—for *The Balcony* and for a number of portraits *(page 79)* that constitute the only record of a friendship that may well have bordered on love. Then, in 1874, Berthe married Manet's brother Eugène, and Édouard never painted her again.

While Manet's fondness for attractive ladies was well known, his discretion was such that we do not know whether the term friendship sometimes did not cover more intimate relations—and this despite the fact that, unlike Berthe Morisot, many of his models were far from being models of virtue. Whatever speculations have been offered about his private life, lack of evidence makes them rumors, no more—and the historian would be well advised to do as did Mme. Manet, who never walked into her husband's studio while he worked.

As Manet's work gained in originality, his father increasingly locked himself up in disapproving silence. His mother sided with Édouard, but out of maternal love rather than conviction. Manet's first commission had been a portrait of Mme. Brunet, a friend of the Manet family. When the picture was finished and the artist showed it to M. and Mme. Brunet, the former was outraged, the latter screamed and wept with horror. Poor Mme. Manet's respectable friends pitied her as one does the mother of an abnormal child. One acquaintance of hers, speaking of *Charlotte Corday*, a hideously vulgar painting by a popular artist, said to a friend: "Look here! This at least has distinction! It isn't like poor Édouard! He is a nice boy, Édouard, but what he paints is so common! It is painful for a woman like Mme. Manet to have a son like that!"

It must have been painful for Manet to *be* a son like that. Sometimes he disapproved of the stir caused by his work as strongly as his father would have. Once, during the scandal about *Olympia*, he sat down in a café; as was the custom, the waiter approached with newspapers—filled with gossip about him. "Who asked you for the newspapers!" Manet snapped at him. In 1865 he had fled to Spain to escape. In 1867 he retreated to Boulogne, on the Channel, to flee from the storm raised by his one-man show. When the mail arrived, bringing the newspapers, he would sigh: "Here comes the flow of mud. The tide is rising." In 1869 he felt the need to run even farther, and that summer he took the steamer from Boulogne to Folkestone. In England, away from his country, he suddenly fancied he could be a prophet. "I believe something can be done here," he wrote to his friend Fantin-Latour. "The land, the atmosphere, everything pleases me, and I shall try to exhibit here next year." And to Zola he reported about British artists: "They do not nurture that kind of ridiculous jealousy which one finds in us; they are almost all gentlemen." But within a week, Manet was back in Boulogne, and never returned to England.

A quick, although superficial, intelligence, a thirst for social life, beautifully dressed women and brilliant gatherings, a penchant for gaiety never trespassing the bounds of good taste, a tendency to be a spendthrift—Édouard Manet seemed the very embodiment of the carefree, idle son of a "good" family. And, after all, he was just that: did he not, in the four years after 1862, when his father died, leaving him a part of his solid fortune, squander the very considerable sum of 80,000 francs? Even his mother found he was going too far when, in 1867, he asked her for 18,000 more to build his exhibition pavilion. "It is time, I think," she warned him, "to stop on this ruinous slope."

To be sure, subtle affinities exist between the man and the artist: the elegance, the quick eye and deep passion for the passing show, for the pleasurable vulnerability of city life were traits shared by both. On the surface, however, the contradictions outweighed the similarities.

He dreamed of being a gentleman-painter. After leaving Couture's school, he shared a studio with just such a rare person, Count Albert de Balleroy, a nobleman who specialized in eminently noble subjects: horse races and hunting scenes. But the conflict between the Dr. Jekyll and the Mr. Hyde in him—or should one say, the Manet and the Fournier?—was too deep. The man and the artist could not be fully reconciled. "Manet is madder than ever," Berthe Morisot's mother once reported to her daughter. He suffered from his contradictions, and the strain to which they subjected him fostered a nervousness that occasionally exploded with a violence quite out of keeping with the amiable, gentle disposition that he customarily displayed. A minor quarrel with the novelist and critic Edmond Duranty so upset him that he provoked his friend to a duel, despite all pleas to calm down. The two met in a deserted wood, at 11 a.m., to fight to the kill; fortunately, the first scratch inflicted by his blade on the writer restored Manet to his senses. He embraced Duranty—and offered him his shoes. Considering the pressures, such outbursts were rare. Like the gentleman he was, Manet carefully hid the sweat and tears from the public.

He knew how to keep a secret. In October 1863 Manet's friends were surprised to hear that he had gone to Holland and returned with a wife. They would have been still more astonished to learn that he had been living with the lady in question for more than 11 years. Around 1850, Suzanne Leenhoff *(page 78)*, a plump, milk-skinned, blue-eyed Dutch pianist, the daughter of an organ player, had come into the Manet household to give the brothers music lessons; Édouard had taken less to the music than to the teacher. He soon set up Suzanne (and her mother) in an apartment and treated her as if she were his wife. His own mother knew about the affair, but his father never did. The rheumatism that paralyzed the elder Manet in his late years mercifully prevented him from getting wind of this unacceptable indignity. Not until his father had died did the artist dare to legitimize his longstanding relationship with Suzanne by marrying her.

Manet's life holds a yet stranger secret. On January 29, 1852, was born, in the words of the Paris birth record, "Léon-Édouard Koëlla, son of Koëlla and of Suzanne Leenhoff." The boy was passed off as the son of Suzanne's mother. Who was Koëlla? Historians have never found the slightest trace of his existence; it seems almost certain that he did not exist. The boy, who appears in many of Manet's pictures, was raised by the latter with truly fatherly care—not unnaturally, for most likely the artist was his father. Yet he never admitted it, nor did he ever legally recognize Koëlla. Manet could not bear scandals.

Manet often sketched Léon Koëlla *(opposite page)*, but this charming crayon study, done in 1865, is the only drawing that bears the boy's name. Léon himself never demonstrated much interest in art. When he grew up, he tried to make a living as a businessman. He dabbled in several ill-conceived ventures, including the founding of a bank that failed, before succeeding with a store that bred and sold chickens, rabbits and fishing worms.

Scandal and Success

Many artists suffer neglect in their times; few artists have had to suffer the brutal critical attacks and the storms of scorn and derision that haunted Manet during the decade following his exhibition of *Luncheon on the Grass*. Hooted at by the public, humiliated in print as an "apostle of the ugly and repulsive," Manet nevertheless went on painting, and between 1863 and 1873 produced some of his most mature, self-confident and daring pictures. These are paintings of the world at large, of the men and women of Paris, of the news events that shook the nation, of the city's entertainments and of the private realm of Manet's friends. During this time of trial he paused to say little in his own defense except to note that "anything containing the spark of humanity, containing the spirit of the age, is interesting."

Countering Manet's antagonists was the one critic who struggled to understand Manet's work and to explain it to others. He was Émile Zola, a novelist who had only recently become an art critic. Zola, whose portrait Manet later painted as a graphic note of thanks, first published a series of newspaper articles and then a pamphlet attacking the "artistic confectioners" of the Salon and pleading for a fair judgment of Manet. "Our fathers laughed at M. Courbet," he wrote, "and now we go into raptures over him. We laugh at M. Manet, and our sons will go into raptures over his canvases. . . . A place is waiting for M. Manet at the Louvre."

Manet posed Zola at a carefully cluttered desk, his pamphlet on the artist peeping out like a signature behind the quill pen. On a bulletin board are pinned examples of the painter's preoccupations; an etching of a Velázquez painting, a Japanese print and what looks like a photograph of Manet's scandalous *Olympia*—looking over at Zola rather than straight out as she does in the actual painting.

Portrait of Émile Zola, 1868

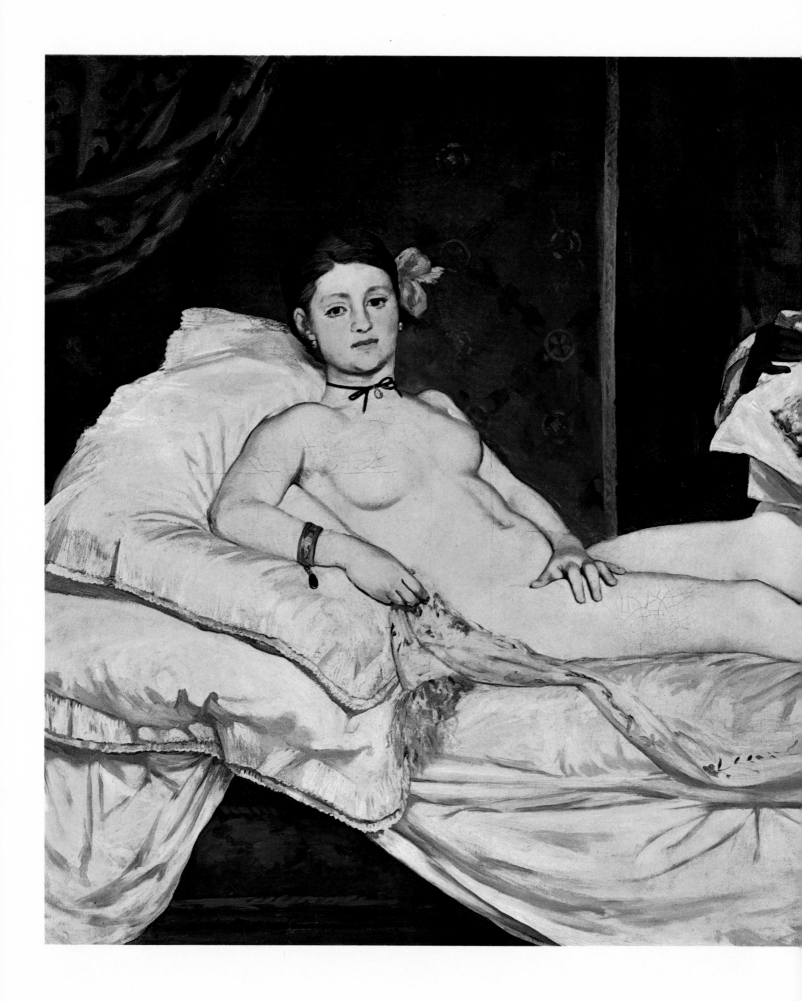

Olympia, 1863

A fter the storm his *Luncheon on the Grass* aroused, Manet waited two years before submitting another nude to the Salon. His *Olympia* was accepted and hung—perhaps because the jury feared that rejection might lead to another Salon des Refusés—but it soon met a cyclone of abuse from both critics and public. Although it was "skyed"—moved to an inconspicuous place high up on a gallery wall—it drew huge crowds of gawkers.

Outraged propriety was the loudest cry against this unprettified Parisienne. Manet had posed his model, Victorine Meurend, as an elegant demimondaine, wearing a black ribbon about her neck, a red orchid in her hair, silk slippers and a gold bracelet, and with a demonic black cat at her feet. Her frank stare challenging the viewer, she disdains the bouquet borne by her maid, a bouquet presumably sent by an admirer who is cooling his heels in another room.

Paradoxically, because they were well acquainted with such women, the Parisians' shrieks of outrage ring false in a city where prostitutes were princesses, where a man's mistress was more likely to be seen in public than his wife and where a perfume of delicious wickedness pervaded the atmosphere. Yet the audience was shocked and would not be calmed even by *Olympia*'s resemblance to Titian's *Venus of Urbino*—which Manet had copied in Italy—and Goya's *The Naked Maja*. Perhaps the reason lies less in Manet's subject than in his unfamiliar style. He forced viewers to look *at* his picture instead of *into* it, as they were used to doing. The space here is extremely shallow, even the couch seems to have no breadth and the colors appear to lie flat on the face of the canvas and only slowly resolve themselves into near and distant objects. In presenting this bold girl in a situation that leaves much to the imagination, and in destroying the traditional boxlike space behind the window of the frame, Manet forces the viewer to work at the picture—to fill out the emotional context and to create in his mind's eye the whole three-dimensional setting. It is this that stunned his audience, and this that makes the picture modern.

71

The Execution of the Emperor Maximilian, 1867-1868

The Battle of the Kearsarge and the Alabama, 1864

Among the events that had all Paris talking during the 1860s were two that Manet painted. In a way, they are pictures of Paris itself, of modern life, and it is appropriate that he needed to paint them.

The American Civil War had long been a topic of interest for Frenchmen when a Confederate privateer, *Alabama*, made a refueling call in Cherbourg. There, she was cornered by the Union corvette, *Kearsarge*, and sunk when she emerged from the harbor. During the long battle, thousands of sightseers watched from the shore and from small boats that flirted about the perimeters of action. Manet himself is alleged to have gone out in one such boat—a notion that lends his painting *(above)* special immediacy.

Paris later buzzed with indignation at the execution of Maximilian, the ill-fated Austrian Archduke who had briefly established an empire in Mexico, supported by an army of French troops. When Napoleon III cravenly withdrew his men at the first protest from the United States, Maximilian was taken by Mexico's republican army and shot. Maximilian (in a large-brimmed hat) and two aides are seen at the instant the deadly bullets are fired. Manet's re-creation, based on documents but also recalling Goya's great firing squad picture *The Third of May, 1808, in Madrid*, strikes home with the detached horror of a news photograph. It is the cool forthrightness in both paintings that caused critics to accuse Manet, wrongly of course, of a lack of sympathy for his subject.

After completing his painting *Concert in the Tuileries*, Manet had found a lively, personal source of subjects in Parisian social life. He and his friend Degas often visited Longchamp, the beautiful race course that had been built in the late 1850s on the reclaimed wastelands west of the city. In his own work Degas would concentrate on the jockeys and the elegant racing animals *(pages 152-153)*. Manet chose as his focus the whole ambiance

THE ART INSTITUTE OF CHICAGO, POTTER PALMER COLLECTION

The Races at Longchamp, Paris, 1864

of the race scene, the bright bustle of the spectators, the neat geometry of the track, the thundering moment when the thoroughbreds pound down the home stretch. Here, under softly clouded skies, a gay crowd presses the rail as the horses drive at the viewer: impressions of the moment are strong; the smell of freshly watered grass is in the air, flickers of light and color strike the eye, the ground trembles from the blurring hooves.

75

The Balcony, 1869

His friends and family frequently served Manet as models. One of his most charming pictures, the idea for which he apparently got while vacationing at the shore in Boulogne, shows in languid poses the young Berthe Morisot *(seated)*, a talented artist who would later marry Manet's brother Eugène, the violinist Fanny Claus and the landscape painter Antoine Guillemet. Dimly seen in the background is Léon Koëlla-Leenhoff, the boy who was probably Manet's natural son. Léon is also the central figure in *The Luncheon (right)*, although portraiture is quite evidently not Manet's intention here. Every element in the picture commands attention: the demure serving girl, the bearded gent, the potted plant—even the armor and saber at the left, which Manet probably added for their curves. But critics continued to misunderstand Manet, and the presence of weapons caused one wag to ask, "Is it a luncheon before or after a duel?"

The Luncheon, 1868

Reading, 1868

One of the reasons given for Manet's frequent use of his family and friends as models is that the continuing critical abuse to which he was subjected led him to turn to a congenial group even for his subjects. Oddly enough, however, there are few paintings of Manet's wife, Suzanne, the woman who had secretly been his mistress for some 11 years before their marriage. In *Reading (above)* she sits by the window in their Paris apartment, her fresh complexion (she was Dutch) and auburn hair set off by the blue-white of her frilled gown and the ruffled curtains behind her; a double necklace of lapis lazuli sharpens the contrast between the crisp fabrics and the smooth, rosy flesh. At the right behind the couch, her son Léon bends over the book he is reading with intense concentration.

Perhaps Manet painted Suzanne so infrequently because he did not find her especially beautiful or interesting to look at. This was evidently not the case with Berthe Morisot, whom he painted many times, in many ways and always wonderfully. The picture at the right, in which his bold blacks leap off the canvas defiantly, is one of his finest. Berthe's penetrating eyes rivet attention on her soft face, framed as it is by the lines of her bonnet strings and the wisps of chestnut hair. Critic Paul Valéry likened this picture to a Vermeer. "But," he wrote, "in Manet's portrait the execution seems more spontaneous, more immediate. The modern man works quickly, he wants to carry out his work before the first impression dies." It is this that makes Manet's pictures everlastingly fresh.

Berthe Morisot with a Bunch of Violets, 1872

IV

The Gang at the Café Guerbois

Looking more like a convocation of bankers than a gathering of avant-garde artists, Manet and a group of friends pose stiffly in the painter's Batignolles studio. Manet is seated at the easel; in profile against the frame on the wall is Renoir; Zola is at Renoir's left and Monet peers shyly out of the right corner. Exhibited at the 1870 Salon, the painting is one of several Fantin-Latour made of his artistic and literary contemporaries.

Henri Fantin-Latour, *Studio at Batignolles*, 1870

"You're as famous as Garibaldi now," the caustic Degas remarked to Manet in 1865. He did not exaggerate, even though Manet's fame, like the Italian revolutionary's, was tinged with more than a slight touch of infamy. People came to Manet's studio, at 81 Rue Guyot, drawn by unhealthy curiosity, as to the scene of a crime. One such visitor was the delicate pre-Raphaelite poet and painter Dante Gabriel Rossetti. "There is a man named Manet," he reported to his mother, "whose pictures are, for the most part, mere scrawls." But if Manet was still derided by those whose approval he yearned for, he did have an enthusiastic following of admirers: the young avant-garde artists who hailed him as the hero who dared to defy the artistic Establishment. Though he was perhaps not altogether pleased by their attention, they boisterously rallied around him. "You are the merry fighter without hatred for anybody, like an old Gaul. I love you for this gaiety even amidst injustice," one member of this rebellious generation, Auguste Renoir, gratefully wrote Manet in 1881. How much more grateful they must have felt in the early 1860s! Another rebel, Camille Pissarro, recalls of those days that when young painters felt discouraged, they would cheer each other up by saying: "Let's go see Manet, he will stand up for us." Without warning or planning, the unassuming, thoroughly undogmatic creator of *Olympia* was made to play the role of master of a school—a role that Fantin-Latour assigns to him in his group portrait, *The Studio at Batignolles (page 80)*.

The meeting place of Manet's "school" was the large, barnlike Café Guerbois. Located on the Grande Rue des Batignolles (now renamed Avenue de Clichy), the Guerbois was conveniently close to Manet's studio and his home, both in the Batignolles quarter, a nondescript district between the fashionable Parc Monceau and the popular Montmartre. Next door the lively restaurant of Père Lathuille exerted a magnetic attraction on the wenches and blades of the neighborhood; across the street was an art-supply store. All this was more than enough incentive for the young writers and painters to set up headquarters around the marble-top tables of the Guerbois. Every afternoon, from five o'clock on, the café filled with the noise of conversation.

Thursday was *the* day for the group. At its center was Manet, gay, informal—his innate distinction showing through a slouchy strut and slangy elocution, which he affected—generous but sometimes sharp-tongued to the point of cruelty. In harsh contrast to his prompt sallies were the slow, ponderous and relentlessly self-assured discourses of his defender, Émile Zola, who was still writing for periodicals and had not yet launched his cycle of epic-scale, naturalistic novels. There were other writers, too. An even earlier defender of Manet, the versatile Zacharie Astruc, sculptor, musician, critic and poet, held forth on the dogmas of Realism. (It was he who had given *Olympia* her name in a burst of mediocre verse celebrating the painting.) The school of Realism was represented also by the mysterious Edmond Duranty, whose every enterprise—from his subtly original, pessimistic novels to his puppet theater in the Tuileries Garden—had been smothered under bad luck; melancholy, soft-spoken, with a touch of bitterness, Duranty forever bit on his unlit pipe. In 1876 he was to write a booklet called *The New Painting,* the first study on the "Batignolles School," as the gossip columnists called the Guerbois group. Also on the scene was Théodore Duret, the cognac dealer and collector whom Manet had encountered in Spain, as well as the critics Philippe Burty and Armand Silvestre.

Artists, however, formed the majority. Manet's old friend, the timid, child-faced Fantin-Latour, plunged apprehensively into the heated atmosphere of the café. Worldly artists like Whistler and Alfred Stevens showed up occasionally. So did Constantin Guys, whose swift, elliptic drawings superbly caught the elegant, dissolute tone of the Second Empire and whose modesty was such that he beseeched Baudelaire, when that poet devoted one of his most profound essays to him, not to mention him by name.

The poet would have had no such request from another of his friends, Félix Tournachon, better known as Nadar. The latter appeared at the Guerbois whenever possible, which, owing to his myriad activ-

"Jesus painting in the midst of his disciples, or Manet's Divine School" is the title of this caricature of Fantin-Latour's famous group portrait of the Batignolles artists *(page 80)*. The inscription at the right is a complicated pun. Appearing to praise Manet, who sits Christlike at the easel, the phrase masks a suggestion that the painter may soon get his comeuppance: "Manet, thou are wit itself . . . a beacon . . ." is a literal translation of the words, but when they are said aloud in French they sound like "Mene, mene, tekel, upharsin"—the Biblical handwriting on the wall. In the Bible story that phrase was interpreted to mean that the destruction of King Belshazzar's wicked reign was imminent.

ities, must have been seldom. His vitality was staggering: Baudelaire jokingly remarked that he had twice as many vital organs as the ordinary person. Cartoonist, novelist, journalist, inventor (he drew plans for a helicopter) and incurable daredevil, Nadar loved celebrity and the company of celebrities. Baudelaire dedicated a poem to him and Manet a painting. Being in the public eye was what the buoyant Nadar loved above all, so he took to ballooning. Jules Verne portrayed him under the name of Ardan (an anagram of Nadar) as one of the astronauts in his book, *From the Earth to the Moon.* Ultimately, however, his fame was to rest chiefly on an activity that he had taken up simply to facilitate his work as a caricaturist: photography. He has given us some of the earliest and finest portraits of the celebrated men and women of his time *(pages 94-95).*

Unlike Nadar, the engraver Félix Bracquemond came regularly, as did, some years later, the picturesque bohemian painter-engraver Marcellin Desboutin. Every evening the latter showed up with his son, a child matured by misery, and his dog; despite his tattered cloak, the father looked unmistakably the grand aristocrat and had, in fact, owned a splendid *palazzo* in Florence before falling into poverty.

At the very core of the Guerbois group was a handful of young radical artists. One of them, in particular, radiated such dedicated passion that he soon came to be regarded as a leader by his contemporaries: Claude Monet *(pages 118-121).* Monet, Manet: the similarity of names at first fooled a great many people, including Manet himself. When Monet's pictures at the Salon of 1865 aroused comment, Manet was furious at what he mistakenly considered to be a usurpation of his name. But he was soon to overcome this initial dislike.

Born in Paris in 1840 and raised in Le Havre, Monet was the son of a grocer. While still in school, he devoted himself to art—or rather to caricature. At 15, his humorous portraits had made him a local celebrity. He might have gotten no further had he not met the painter Eugène Boudin. The latter's intense observation of the play of light and air on the sea *(pages 54-55)* gave his work a fresh and improvisational quality that was unusual in the late 1850s. Won over to nature by his admiration for Boudin, Monet was inspired to go to Paris in 1859 to study landscape. At once, he rejected the discipline of the École des Beaux-Arts and chose to work on his own at the Atelier Suisse, which Manet had also attended. His studies were interrupted when he was conscripted and sent to Algeria for his military service. After two years Monet returned from North Africa, his eyes filled with indelible impressions of what was one day to become his prime inspiration: the sun.

But it was too soon for such brilliance; instead, Monet entered the studio run by the Beaux-Arts professor and landscapist Charles Gleyre. Gleyre's chief merit as a teacher was tolerance, a virtue much needed in the case of a student for whom the heart of learning consisted in unlearning. Traditional painting, Monet felt, interposed smoked glasses between his eyes and the dazzling message of nature. "The more I advance, the more I regret what little I know; that is what bothers me

Claude Monet, as a youth, was more apt to fill the pages of his school notebook with caricatures than with lessons. This sketch of his art teacher, Mario Ochard, displays a drawing skill and a satirical eye of remarkable sophistication for a boy not yet 18. Monet's early talents are all the more interesting in that neither careful delineation nor the sense of humor is evident in his mature work.

most." New encouragement came when, in Le Havre, he met Johan-Barthold Jongkind, the Dutch seascapist in whom the qualities of freshness and freedom of vision possessed by Boudin were raised to a higher pitch of incandescence. "I owe him," Monet later acknowledged, "the final education of my eye."

Monet's eye: what a formidably sensitive seeing machine! "Nothing but an eye—but what an eye!" his colleague Cézanne said of Monet. His problem, in the 1860s, was how to render what he saw. His eye was far ahead of his hand. To close the gap, he painted outdoors more and more (even landscapists like Corot did most of their work in the studio). But the old indoor attitudes and devices were not easily shrugged off. Monet groped, failed, frequently destroying his paintings, only to start again, with the indomitable energy that was to make him execute more than 3,000 canvases in the course of his 86 years. And exerting a decisive influence on the work of his exploratory period were the artistic courage, the reliance on personal vision rather than school recipes, the abrupt contrasts of shadow and light, and the simplifications of his older friend, Manet.

Matters were further complicated for Monet by his poverty. With his model and mistress Camille, he suffered through frequent periods of hunger and despair, and once even tried to commit suicide. Such was his state of misery that he was forced, in 1867, to return to his aunt's home near Le Havre even though his family required that he abandon Camille, then pregnant. When she gave birth to a son, Jean, later that year, Monet was too destitute to buy a train ticket back to Paris. The next winter found Claude, Camille and Jean together in the capital, still desperately poor. His friend Renoir stole bread from his mother's table so Monet would be able to eat.

Auguste Renoir (*pages 122-125*) too was a regular at the Guerbois. A thin, nervous youth with mobile eyes and a lively manner, he was usually bored with the discussions on esthetics, but was happy to sit in the protective shade of Monet, his inseparable friend. He painted as the nightingale sings; nightingales need branches on which to rest, and Monet was Renoir's moral support. "Without him, I would have given up," Renoir confessed. Born in Limoges, the porcelain capital, in 1841, he early showed artistic inclinations, and his father, a tailor, sensibly apprenticed him to a porcelain decorator; the glazed transparency of his mature paintings owes much to this early training. After decorating pottery, he decorated fans, finding motifs in the art of his 18th Century predecessors Watteau, Boucher and Fragonard. Their rosy, carefree, sensuous hymns to womanhood left an indelible mark on him: woman was to be his chief artistic concern. "If God hadn't created woman," he once exclaimed, "I don't know whether I would have become a painter!" When men posed for him, even they acquired an indefinably feminine quality; and he lent to landscape something of the tender succulence of a woman's flesh.

In 1862, along with Monet, Renoir entered the studio of Gleyre, who was shocked by his lack of "seriousness." "No doubt it is to have fun that you paint?" Gleyre asked him superciliously. "But of course," Renoir replied with candor; "if it weren't fun, you may be sure that I wouldn't do it!" Nightingales do not sing well in cages; for Renoir, school was a cage. He reacted against it by looking toward Courbet, whose opulent women were congenial to him; but above all, he turned to Monet, in whose company he frequently lived, painted and labored to attain pictorial freedom.

Monet's friendly authority also influenced two other Gleyre students, Bazille and Sisley. Born in the same year as Renoir, Jean-Frédéric Bazille came from a prosperous family of wine growers. He was sent to Paris to study medicine, but, like so many of his comrades at the Guerbois, he upset his family's plans for him. Deeply impressed by Monet, he chose to paint men and women in *plein air*—i.e., outdoors. But whereas, in Monet's work, light demonstrated its supremacy by penetrating all shapes, in Bazille's paintings it remains accessory, external —a kind of studio lighting, stronger than heretofore, but cast on a world of unchanged, classical order.

Bazille was an habitué of the Guerbois, where Zola observed him: "Blond, tall and thin, very distinguished. Looking a bit like Jesus, but manly, very handsome." Sudden fits of rage would flush his pale complexion, yet his kindness was extreme. Richer than his friends, he helped them as much as he could, giving them shelter, buying their canvases, even placing his scanty medical experience at their service (to make Monet rest an injured leg, he forced him to pose for a picture lying in bed).

The fourth member of the Monet contingent was Alfred Sisley *(pages 130-131)*. Born in France of British parents in 1839, he had entered Gleyre's studio at about the same time as Monet, Renoir and Bazille. There, as at the Guerbois, it was easy not to notice him. Shy, withdrawn, he seldom joined in the conversation. Yet he thought and expressed himself with great clarity, and he was endowed with the kind of intelligence that consists in knowing one's true nature and limits. His artistic virtues were freshness and integrity of vision, extreme delicacy and sensitiveness of eye and hand. It is not surprising that he was drawn to the modest, incomparably subtle landscapes of Corot. The frail, muted melody of Sisley's art required quiet and seclusion; he spent most of his time in the country and concentrated on landscape.

Another disciple of Corot was the robust, outgoing Camille Pissarro *(pages 126-129)*. Born in 1830 on St. Thomas in the West Indies, Pissarro had gone off to school in Paris, then returned to work in his family's general store. After running away to Venezuela with a Danish artist he met on the waterfront, Pissarro finally persuaded his parents to let him return to Paris and become a painter. Influenced first by Corot and later by Courbet, he had a sense of the unbudging massiveness of earth that was not to desert him even when he joined Monet and his friends in their dizzying quest of elusive light.

The same reassuring solidity radiated from Pissarro's sturdy, bearded figure as he held forth, with quiet tenacity, at the Guerbois. Older than most of his comrades by nearly a decade—and two years senior even to Manet—he was a kindly fanatic who firmly believed in progress, whether in science, politics or the arts. Indeed, he thought that all revolutions went hand in hand. Politically, he was a Socialist of the anarchist variety. (He was a social rebel, too: he lived with and then married his mother's maid. She bore him seven children, including five sons who all became painters.)

Driven by an abiding love for his fellow men, Pissarro believed that talent should be shared. Nobody was more willing to teach others, and he did so with magnificent conviction, clarity and unselfishness. "He was such a professor that he could have taught stones to draw correctly," said the American painter Mary Cassatt. Truly open-minded, he achieved something harder still than teaching his juniors: he allowed himself to learn from them. Even more helpful than his lessons was his presence. He gave confidence to the anguished, the doubting, the tormented. "Pissarro was humble and colossal, something like God the Father," recalled Paul Cézanne, the first in a line of Pissarro protégés that was also to include Gauguin and Armand Guillaumin.

Cézanne had followed his schoolmate Zola from Aix-en-Provence to Paris to study art. Despite the anger of his father, a tyrannical, provincial hat-manufacturer grown wealthy, Cézanne had given up the law for the easel. In turn rebellious and cowed before paternal authority, Cézanne compensated for his shyness and frustration, both in his life and his work, by extreme aggressiveness. Had it not been for Pissarro, whom he had met at the Atelier Suisse and whose stabilizing influence was to help him find his way, he might not have been accepted by the Guerbois group. Deliberately uncouth in dress and in speech, he occasionally broke his surly silence with violent exclamations. Entering the café, he would hitch up his pants and gruffly shake everybody's hand—except Manet's, to whom he said: "I won't shake your hand, M. Manet, since I haven't washed in a week."

Nothing could be more striking than the contrast between Cézanne and Edgar Degas *(pages 150-167)*, who completed the inner circle of the Guerbois group. Cool, punctilious, aloof, hidden behind a barricade of egotism whence he unleashed the arrows of a deadly irony, Degas was the closest to Manet in age, upbringing and artistic concerns—no doubt the reason why the two carried on the intermittent war of innuendo, nasty quips and quarrels that shadowed their lifelong friendship from the day of their meeting in the Louvre. Degas was born in 1834 in an apartment located above the Paris branch of the Neapolitan bank founded by his grandfather. His father was a highly cultured bourgeois, a connoisseur of music and the arts, on friendly terms with some of France's most discerning collectors. When young Edgar displayed a gift for drawing, he found full understanding and encouragement at home.

A student of an Ingres disciple, permeated with the message of the Italian Renaissance, deeply attached to the past, he had, like Manet, considerable trouble in coming to artistic terms with the reality of his day. As late as 1865, he chose to exhibit at the Salon a historical picture dealing with a medieval episode, *The Misfortunes of the City of Orléans.* Although he was a regular at the Guerbois, Degas enjoyed no less the company of conservative painters like Léon Bonnat. He made contact with contemporary subject matter through portraiture but did not strike a truly modern chord until he turned to two themes that he was to investigate so stubbornly that they remain indissolubly attached to his name: horse races and ballet dancers.

The latter—with their taut counterpoint of aerial performance and earthly performer—illustrated Degas' deepest convictions: that art was a brilliant artifice, perfected through will power and intelligence, and that women, once one probed beyond the seductive mask and pose, were grotesque. Degas was a misogynist who used pencil and brush as scalpels to pierce life's graces and ferret out the secrets and intimacies that lurked backstage and behind closed doors. He treated his subjects provided by the contemporary world—seamstresses, milliners or men about town—like a surgeon probing for malignancy.

And that was also why Degas needed the Guerbois and its crowd. Exceedingly intelligent and neurotic, Degas, his sensuous mouth strangely denied by his icy eyes, found cruelty an easy way to make contact with the outside world. As his art dealer Paul Durand-Ruel once pointedly remarked: "That man knew only one pleasure: to get mad at somebody." At the café, with its radical, argumentative patrons, there was ample opportunity.

Had it been the "right" thing for proper women to go to cafés, Berthe Morisot would probably have been seen at the Guerbois. But she was far too well-bred. Spiritually, though, she shared the Guerbois habitués' passionate interest in the new message of painting. Corot had instructed her and her less talented sister Edma, and it was Fantin-Latour who introduced the young ladies to Manet during one of those sessions of copying that turned the Louvre—in every sense of the term—into a veritable drawing room. "I agree with you," Manet had jokingly written his friend some time later, "the demoiselles Morisot are charming. Too bad they are not men. However, as women, they might serve the cause of painting by each marrying an academician and by sowing the seeds of discord in the ranks of those senile fellows. But that would be asking of them great self-sacrifices indeed."

As she sat for and worked with Manet, Berthe absorbed his artistic message. She translated it into personal terms: less powerful, more intimate, with an ebullient lightness of touch quite her own, but reminiscent of Fragonard (to whom she was remotely related). A strong, independent personality, she nevertheless showed characteristically feminine jealousy when Manet took on his one and only student in the strict sense, Eva Gonzalès. He had been attracted by Eva's plump beauty and also, one may guess, by the fact that she was a deserter from the studio of the slick and successful society portraitist Chaplin. Artistically, Berthe Morisot had little cause for jealousy: whereas she freely interpreted Manet's lessons, Eva Gonzalès was an obedient but rather uninventive student.

How exciting they were, those smoke-and-noise-filled evenings at the Guerbois! Long after, Monet recalled them fondly. "Nothing was more interesting than these discussions, with their perpetual clash of opin-

Berthe Morisot *(below)* was recognized as a fine painter by both the Impressionists, many of whom were her close friends, and the Salon juries that accepted her work. In 1874 she married Manet's brother Eugène. Their only child, Julie, became one of her mother's favorite subjects—the sketch above was made when Julie was 11. In her lifetime Julie knew not only Manet, but Monet, Renoir and Rodin, among others. As a wedding present, Degas gave her the sketches of her Uncle Édouard shown on page 6.

ions. They kept one's spirit awake, encouraged one to disinterested and sincere research, enabled one to store away reserves of enthusiasm, which nourished one for weeks and weeks." Considering the extreme disparities in character, background, political conviction and artistic purpose of its members, the existence of the group for almost a decade from its inception around 1866 seems close to miraculous. This motley, explosive crew was kept together by solidarity in the face of nearly universal hostility. Most of them were, at one time or another, refused by the jury of the Salon. "I believe," wrote Manet in a letter to Fantin-Latour, "that if we would stick together and, above all, not lose courage, it would be possible to react against this mediocre world, whose only strength lies in its unity."

But the Guerbois coalition was cemented also by more positive ties. Though they may seem diametrically opposed, the coloristic landscapes of Monet and the linear studies of men and women in action by Degas possessed a common artistic creed. It is summarized by the original title of another of Fantin-Latour's group pictures, *The Toast:* "To truth, our ideal." All the Guerbois painters believed that the duty of artists was to render faithfully, without allegory or fictionalizing, what they saw about them. "All I did was to look," Monet put it. In short, their purpose did not differ substantially from that of Courbet or from the literary goals of the writers of the group—Astruc, Duranty and Zola—who were all ardent advocates of Realism.

The difference between Courbet's Realism and that of the Batignolles School was that though they looked at the same world, the younger artists saw it with sharper eyes and looked at it in broad daylight instead of through the dark filter of the studio. As a result, they saw more and what they saw was cast in a wider range of light and color.

Gradually, however, the appearance of reality was transformed by the close observation that the painters devoted to it. Just as a drop of water, which looks inert when viewed with the naked eye, discloses all manner of agitation when seen through the microscope, so the probing attention of the new Realists discovered that reality was not stable, but in perpetual flux. Time and motion were as much factors of reality as were mass and place. Fashion, the time of day, modify a girl's aura the way the sun's course alters the look of a field. What is true one moment no longer holds the next. To be faithful "to truth, our ideal," therefore, required that one capture the fleeting instant. Courbet himself had sensed this. Once, the painter Daubigny had complimented him on a study of the sea. "It is not a study of the sea," Courbet had replied, "it is a moment in time." This was truer still for Boudin's deft pastel studies of sky and ocean—Baudelaire claimed they were so precise you could tell the season and hour of their execution. The growing use of a sketchy manner instead of a meticulous finish rose out of the need to evolve a swift, stenographic idiom capable of keeping up with changing reality.

With Monet, the search for the moment became a method. In the year of his death, 1926, he summarized his lifetime's work as the endeavor to paint "directly from nature, striving to render my impression in the face of the most fugitive effects." On another occasion, he stated that "what I seek is instantaneity," and to this end he deliberately pitted himself against the most unstable aspects of landscape: the fluidity of water and the perpetual motion of light.

Motion was Degas' concern also—galloping horses, ballerinas going through their paces. Bodily motion is a succession of moments of unstable equilibrium, a constantly reshuffled equation of forces. Degas' aim was to capture the precise instant when such an equation is formulated by the mechanism of human or animal limbs. This instant is best caught by the precision of photography, and Degas was fascinated with this new medium (*pages 98-99*), which since its development in the 1830s had attracted wide attention in France.

"Instantaneity is photography," he said. A number of the compositional devices used by Degas in his paintings irresistibly call to mind photography: the unusual perspectives (plunging or steeply ascending), the abrupt cutting off of a form by the picture's edge, the air of arbitrariness, even of random selection, such as the world takes on in front of the candid camera. Actually, in his case it was more a matter of foreseeing the implications of photography rather than actually imitating them, for technically photography was still in its infancy in the 1860s, and it still strove to imitate painting. When speed photography developed—Degas owned one of the first Kodaks—its vision seemed borrowed from Degas' art.

Other painters were interested in photography as well. Ingres and Delacroix had toyed with it, and so did Manet. The strange unrelatedness of the figures in pictures like *The Balcony* is like that produced by the dispassionate eye of the camera—which recalls nothing but what a given moment places before it. The figures' inexpressiveness reminds one of the blank stare with which one responds to the sudden intrusion of that stranger, the photographer. Manet, too, was deeply concerned with instantaneity: like Degas, he devoted a whole series of studies in crayon, gouache and oil to the tumult of thoroughbreds racing toward the post at Longchamp. In such sketches, he developed a breathtakingly prompt, cursive, elliptic manner, which enabled him to catch the essence of the passing scene.

But for Manet, unlike his friends of the Guerbois, instantaneity was not an end. His concern was the vision provoked by the flash of recognition, not the flashbulb view. He sensed that a second of time was like a shell enclosing the vivid kernel of immediate experience. To get at this moment of pure presence when, freed from the weight of dead memories and routines, one's awareness fuses with the object that confronts it, one must split the second. In this, he differed radically from the rest of the group: while they sought to deal with the transience of an instant of reality, he struggled to capture its essential nature.

Yet Manet felt this difference obscurely, if at all. Of his artistic aims, he spoke much as the others did: "One must be of one's time," he affirmed. Or again: "One must paint what one sees." Years later—the Batignolles School had by now deserted the Café Guerbois—when he organized an exhibition of his paintings in his own studio, Manet put an inscription on the invitation card that echoes the one on Fantin-Latour's *The Toast:* "Paint the truth, and do not worry about what people say." Manet, in short, saw himself as a Realist.

And so did his "gang." Nobody, not even his closest friends, recognized that he was basically different. For them, he was a new link in the chain of visual progress; he had gone a great step further than Courbet in the direction of the complete rendition of modern life. He had dared to open the windows of the studio and—so his admirers claimed —let the sun drench the canvas. In this, he *was* the master of the younger, at that time slower-moving, Realists from Monet to Degas.

But progress is a continuous chain. The same attitude that made the younger generation hail Manet as a more advanced Realist than Courbet was bound, someday, to make them see their own, perfected brand of observation as superseding his. That day was not far off—by 1868 or 1869, Monet, Renoir, Pissarro and Degas were on the verge of maturity and a new adventure in art was about to begin. But it would have to wait for a bit; France was about to be plunged into a national tragedy.

On July 15, 1870, Bismarck at last achieved the aim of his imperialistic aspirations: he goaded France into declaring war against Prussia. The French armies, disorganized, demoralized, wretchedly equipped and poorly led, suffered defeat upon defeat, which culminated, on September 2, with the disaster of Sedan in northern France, where Napoleon III, with 100,000 men, was taken prisoner. Léon Gambetta, a republican member of the National Assembly, took over the reins of government and strove to organize French resistance. It was a colossal task, for the victorious Prussian forces lost no time in occupying province after province north of the Loire River. By September 19, Paris was cut off from the rest of the country and was girding itself for the trials of a protracted siege.

Degas was in Paris, as was Manet, who had wisely sent away his mother, wife and the boy Koëlla to the safe, distant South. The two friends enlisted in the artillery. As far as Manet was concerned, it was primarily a gesture. Much of his military activity, according to Berthe Morisot (who had bravely refused, despite Manet's entreaties, to take flight), consisted in changing into dress uniform. As a lieutenant in the National Guard, he served at headquarters, under the orders, ironically enough, of none other than the artistic hero of the academicians, Colonel Ernest Meissonier.

Soon food began to grow scarce in the beleaguered capital. "The turn of horses has come; donkey is now a prince's dish," Manet wrote to his wife. (It was Nadar's balloons that carried the mail—as well as Gambetta himself—over the German lines to unoccupied territory.) A few weeks later, another distinguished Parisian, Victor Hugo, noted in his diary: "It is no longer even horse meat that we are eating. *Perhaps* it is dog meat. *Perhaps* it is rats? I am beginning to have stomach pains. We eat the unknown." Nor did the zoo animals escape the common fate. "The elephant of the Jardin des Plantes has been slaughtered," noted Hugo on January 2, 1871. "It wept. It will be eaten." Bitter cold compounded the sufferings of hunger. Nevertheless, Parisians bravely resisted in the hope that the new armies raised by Gambetta would deliver them. They turned danger into distraction. "The Parisians, out of curiosity, go to see the bombed districts. One looks at bombs as one would look at fireworks," wrote Hugo.

But the high spirits were only a gallant façade. "All this is very sad," Manet wrote, "for the outcome can only be fatal to us." And somewhat later: "We sit down at the table only by force of habit." Life had become, in Manet's word, "unbearable." Starved and frozen, its last hope of liberation crushed, and rent by internal dissension, Paris capitulated on January 28, 1871. Less than two months later, it was to experience the even uglier horrors of civil war.

Parisians, despairing of conditions in their city, dissatisfied with the surrender terms and exasperated by bungled administration, drove the leaders of the national government into "exile" in Versailles just outside Paris and established a communal government. The Versailles group raised an army and laid siege to Paris for the second time in a few months, while the Prussian victors remained neutral observers. Finally the Commune was crushed, and the streets ran with the blood of 17,000 Communards and suspected sympathizers killed in ferocious reprisals.

With peace, news of the Guerbois group began to arrive. Manet, weakened by the siege of Paris and deeply depressed by political events, joined his family in the Pyrenees. Of some the news was bad. Bazille had been killed at the front on November 28, 1870. Renoir had been drafted into the cuirassiers, sent to Bordeaux and thence to the Pyrenees, where he contracted so severe a case of dysentery that he was given up for lost. Having miraculously recovered, he returned to Paris in time to witness the tragedy of the Commune. Cézanne's patriotic feelings were notably less evident: to escape the draft, he left his parents' home in Aix-en-Provence to live in seclusion in the hills of L'Estaque, near Marseilles, overlooking the Mediterranean.

Both Monet and Pissarro were convinced socialists; when the war broke out, they felt under no obligation to fight for the Empire, which they hated. When Pissarro fled to London, the German quartermaster corps set up a butcher shop in his house at Louveciennes and trampled many of his canvases to destruction. Monet, leaving his wife and child in the care of Boudin at Le Havre, also escaped to London. So disrupted was communication in France that it was quite by chance that the two friends met in London. There, they also met the landscapist Daubigny, who generously introduced them to his dealer, Paul Durand-Ruel. It was he who would, in a few years, provide the material support that made it possible for the new art to survive.

For the flame kindled at the Café Guerbois had not been snuffed out altogether. In London, Monet and Pissarro continued to paint. The discovery of the work of Constable and Turner confirmed and strengthened their convictions about the importance of a fresh vision and the role of light in painting. When the war ended, and Monet and Pissarro returned to France, the flame had grown into a fire that was soon to spread to the rest of the group: Impressionism was about to be born.

Manet caught the brutality of a street firing squad during the last days of the Paris Commune in the lithograph called *The Barricade*. Returning from the south in May 1871, he found the city as an English reporter described it: "Paris the beautiful is Paris the ghastly, Paris the battered, Paris the burning, Paris the blood-spattered, now."

Photography: A New Vision

In 1839 L. J. M. Daguerre's disclosure of the secret process by which he had collaborated with the sun to record an image on a silvered sheet of copper—the first workable and permanent photographic method—aroused Paris to a frenzy of *Daguerreotypomania*. Almost overnight photography became the most popular invention of the century. It doomed the careers of some painters—those who specialized in small, meticulous, expensive portrait miniatures in particular—and it provoked traditionalists to angry condemnation of this "mechanical plagiarism of nature," which they saw as a pretentious rival incapable of expressing the spiritual realm of art. But to the growing band of rebellious modernists, photography became not only a valued accessory but an inspiration.

Painters as diverse in their styles as Ingres, Delacroix and Manet found that they could often do away with tedious portrait sittings or long, arduous poses of models by painting from photographs of their subjects, some of which they made themselves. (Delacroix was a charter member of the French Heliographic Society.) Artists who, like Degas, were interested in picturing motion used stop-action photographs to see the reality that their eyes could not catch. But more than as a mere tool, photography served art by creating a large and visually sophisticated audience and by providing painters, who were already beginning to break out of the old molds, with new perceptions of the visible world.

This historic photograph, the earliest known daguerreotype,
was made by Daguerre in his studio in 1837,
two years before he announced his technique to the world.

Honoré Daumier

Gustave Courbet

Nadar's aerial photograph of the Étoile district of Paris.

Édouard Manet

The most famous name in mid-century photography was Nadar, the flashy pseudonym of Gaspard Félix Tournachon, a dabbler at painting, a journalist and a popular caricaturist who established the most fashionable portrait studio in Paris. There, at 35 Boulevard des Capucines, he welcomed the rich, the notable and the artistic, as they sat for such psychologically probing likenesses as those reproduced here of Daumier, Courbet and Manet. A friend to the new, Nadar often met and argued with the rebels of painting, to whom, in 1874, he rented his studio for the first exhibition of Impressionism.

Nadar was a bold innovator himself. In 1856 he went aloft in a balloon over Paris and made the world's first aerial photograph. Four years later, in the sewers and catacombs beneath the city's streets, he became one of the first to make photographs using artificial light. Artists called him the "Titian of photography."

Madame Nadar posed with her aeronaut husband in a balloon basket safely suspended in the studio.

Retouchers and colorists were as much a fixture in a photographer's studio as the velvet posing chair, fancy frames and scenic backgrounds.

Within a decade after Daguerre revealed his process, improved methods and equipment made lifelike portraiture so easy and so fashionable that hundreds of painters of miniature portraits went out of business. By 1849, some 100,000 Parisians were having their pictures taken every year.

At first, the public was fascinated by the complete objectivity with which the camera could view its subject. But when it came to their own portraits, many grew disenchanted with the camera's too-perfect fidelity to detail, exposing as it did every blemish, wrinkle and imperfection. Skillful posing and artful lighting could camouflage only so much, and thus, by a curious paradox, the very portrait painters who had been displaced were once more in demand as retouchers of unflattering photographs. Color, at first added for realism, soon

Count de Brazza, the heroic explorer of the Congo, posed on a cardboard rock at Nadar's.

became cosmetic; standards of male and female beauty were published in photographic journals as guides in the correction of physical defects; the retoucher was even empowered to trim a bit off a lady's waistline after his own idea of a good figure.

Painters also came back into the photographer's studio to prepare scenic backdrops and artful props with which the photographer was now forced to surround his more demanding patrons. In crowded, busy, skylit studios like the one above, with its painted canvas antique column, forest and bookcase lined against the back wall, dozens of clients might pose for their portraits of a morning, selecting elegant oval frames and ordering prints before departing. By organizing the efforts of his crew of retouchers and assistants, the proprietor of one such studio turned out an estimated 2,400 prints in a day.

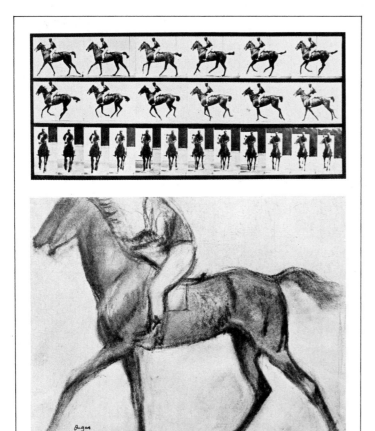

Degas sketched the second frame of a Muybridge sequence.

Among the few enlightened painters who realized the true value of photography was Edgar Degas. Degas had been drawing and painting horses—he was fascinated with their power and elegant movement—for almost two decades when photographer Eadweard Muybridge finally showed, through a series of stop-action still photographs, how horses really moved. Like everyone else, Degas was amazed, for Muybridge's pictures *(top left)* proved that a horse's feet leave the ground in a rolling sequence, not in the "hobbyhorse" pairs that most artists pictured. Degas' sketch of one of Muybridge's stills enabled him to better understand the action of cantering.

Degas also worked directly from a photograph in painting the portrait at left below. And he posed the photograph at the lower right as a joke, poking fun at a famous painting by Ingres.

The pose and elusive expression of a widely circulated photograph of Princess Metternich reappear in a Degas portrait.

A fine draftsman himself, Degas admired the proficiency of Ingres' *Apotheosis of Homer (above)*, but poked fun at the stiff, static quality of the painting by imitating it with the photograph below.

Lampooning Ingres' painting, Degas posed himself as the central figure in the photograph.

Perhaps what photography contributed most to painting was an enlarged vocabulary of seeing: dramatic perspectives such as that in the view of the Paris boulevard at right; bold compressions of depth between figures in a scene and between figures and background; the blurring or freezing of action; and the brutal and often arbitrary cutting off of a part of a figure or an object by the edge of the photograph. But most important of all in this new understanding of the visual world was the sense of the instantaneous, of the fleeting impression of reality frozen for all time. It was this, above all, that would become the chief preoccupation of the Impressionist painters and endure as a quality of much modern art.

These new approaches to picture-making, so different from the formulas for well-ordered, well-balanced, time*less* compositions of much academic painting, might have come forth from artists working independently. But certainly photography speeded up the process of discovery, acting as a kind of catalyst.

In the end, far from causing the death of painting, as some feared photography would, or forcing painting to give up depicting "reality" —which it was thought photography could do much better—the craft of the camera evolved its own artists and its own esthetics. And in the process, it revitalized painting, forcing redefinitions of old concepts, urging new perceptions of the world and creating a huge, new audience that took pleasure in seeing.

French photographers Ferrier and Solier made this "instantaneous" view in 1860. Millions like it were sold each year.

V

The Flowering
of Impressionism

To the easily shocked Parisians of
1868, this lithograph of two
amorous cats stalking each other
on a rooftop seemed scandalously
suggestive. It was a poster created
by Manet to advertise a chatty
book about cats by his friend
Champfleury. Done in flat, broad
areas of black and white, in a style
reminiscent of Japanese woodcuts
(which Manet knew and admired),
the lithograph was one of several
that Manet made to illustrate
Champfleury's text.

The Cats' Meeting, 1868

"Ah! the beautiful, calm, varied and stinking river, full of mirages
and filth." Guy de Maupassant was talking about the Seine, which,
around 1860, had become a favorite playground of Parisians. On week-
ends, gay bands of lightly dressed girls and mustachioed men wearing
striped shirts and straw hats would descend upon the dozens of riv-
erside restaurants within easy reach of the city. Sailing and rowing were
the rage, and remained so until the bicycle dethroned them, about 1890.
Maupassant, a fanatic canoeist, has left us a glowing picture of those
sun-drenched days: "How many amusing things and funny girls I saw
during the days I spent canoeing! . . . a life of strength and carelessness,
of gaiety and poverty, of robust and boisterous merrymaking!" The era
had a distinctly amiable notion of sport, and it definitely implied the
presence of women—delicate women, of course, so as not to weigh
down the fragile craft. "A woman is something indispensable in a boat,"
Maupassant explains. "Indispensable because she keeps mind and heart
awake, because she stimulates, amuses, distracts, lends spice, and com-
pletes the scenery with a red umbrella gliding by the green banks."

Surely, this description has brought a score of pictures to the read-
er's mind—pictures, signed by Monet, Renoir, Sisley, Manet, that
constitute the quintessence of the movement known to us as Impressionism. This is no accident, for it was at a popular haven for boaters,
Argenteuil, on the Seine, that Impressionism came into its own and
achieved its finest flowering.

Monet went there first in 1871. He was joined that summer and for
several summers following by Renoir and Sisley. Manet, of course, had
been spending part of the summers there most of his life, at his family's
property in nearby Gennevilliers. He painted with his younger colleagues and in 1874, when Monet was threatened by eviction from his
house, found him another place to live in Argenteuil. Other painters of
the Guerbois group also moved to the country. Pissarro settled first at
Louveciennes, then at Pontoise (both small country towns within 25
miles of Paris), where his protégé, Cézanne, followed him. Sisley was
later to live at Moret-sur-Loing, on a small tributary of the Seine. The

immediate motive for their move was practical: it was cheaper to live outside Paris and they were all desperately poor. But they were also inspired by motives that were not just practical. In the country they could practice what they preached: landscape painting out of doors.

Despite the efforts of Corot and the Barbizon painters, a devotion to landscape painting was still, to the established art world, a contemptible credo. As one Salon review put it, echoing the École's dogma on landscape art: "It is a genre that ought not to exist." A landscape was acceptable only as the setting of an action; without it, it seemed as uninteresting as a stage without performers. It was because this criticism was so deeply rooted in the early 19th Century mind that Corot did not exhibit a pure landscape at the Salon until 1849, though he had been painting them for more than a quarter of a century. Landscape, in short, remained the proletarian among the genres of painting.

As for painting outdoors—a serious painter would never have been caught there. Nature was re-created from sketches or laboriously made models. "When I painted my *Retreat from Russia*," Meissonier told an American visitor who asked about the snowy vistas, "instead of boric acid I used powdered sugar. What a snow effect I had achieved! But it had attracted the bees of a nearby hive. I therefore replaced the sugar with flour. Whereupon it was mice that invaded my battlefield. I ended by wondering whether I would not be reduced to waiting for a snowfall to paint a winter landscape."

This attitude explains why the painters who took their landscape seriously and who did go outdoors to look at it were the pariahs of the art world. They were either pantheists like Théodore Rousseau or socialists and humanitarians like Daubigny, Millet and Courbet. To them, nature was a way of life. Daily, intimate contact with it caused them to pay ever greater attention to the real look of the outdoors and to the factors that affected it—above all, light. (Years later Manet would remark, "Light is the principal personage of a painting.")

This thirst for truth drove landscapists to take daily walks through the countryside and eventually, in the 1860s, to set up their easels in its midst. Yet while Realism provided the conscious motive for this rush to field and wood, there was also an unconscious one. The landscapist, noted Rousseau, "lives in silence." Years later, Cézanne was to emphasize the very same aspect: "The countryside is truly astonishing. It seems there is more silence here." Now silence—the hushing of anecdote—was precisely the ever-stronger aspiration of painting in the 19th Century. By providing artists with mute subject matter, nature proved a reliable ally in their struggle for a new type of painting emancipated from storytelling. As a result, the lowly genre of landscape, together with still life—which we might call the indoor version of landscape—became the "hot" sector of painting during the last third of the century.

Until the 1870s, Barbizon had been the mecca for landscapists. Monet's move to Argenteuil and the Seine held special significance. To be sure, it bespoke a love of the water that could be expected of a man brought up by the seaside—Monet once declared that he would like to

When French landscape painters began seeking inspiration in the countryside in the 1830s they made Barbizon, in the great forest of Fontainebleau, their headquarters. Partly inspired by these pioneers—Corot, Millet, Daubigny—the Impressionists went outdoors, often finding suitable sites within a short radius of Paris. River and seaside locales were especially favored, and the names Auvers, Pontoise, Argenteuil, Sainte-Adresse and Honfleur will be found again and again on their light-struck canvases.

be buried in a buoy. He and his friends had a passion for boats. A few years earlier, Sisley and Renoir had sailed down the Seine to Le Havre. At Argenteuil, Manet introduced Monet to a young naval architect, also president of the local yacht club, Gustave Caillebotte, who advised the artist on the construction of a boat. Under the influence of his new friends, Caillebotte, an amateur painter, decided to make art his profession; but he proved most useful to them as one of their earliest and most enthusiastic collectors.

Boats were merely part of the story. Unlike the Barbizon painters or Courbet, who were concerned with the stable reality of nature, Manet's friends were seeking to capture the unstable, fugitive aspects of landscape. A river was not only nature at its most fluid—"we can never bathe twice in the same river" wrote the Greek philosopher Heraclitus —but it also provided the artists with a very special way of looking at fluidity, of seeing instability.

The mechanics of vision, in fact, was one of the chief concerns of Manet and his friends. A French chemist, Eugène Chevreul, director of the dyeing department of the Gobelins tapestry factory in Paris, had in the first half of the century conducted a series of experiments that led to an influential book, *The Principles of Harmony and Contrast of Colors and Their Application to the Arts.* He demonstrated that juxtaposed colors affect each other. Every color leaves behind a visual sensation, an afterimage of its complementary color. Hence, when one dab of color is laid next to another of its complementary color, they brighten each other; conversely, it is possible for two neighboring colors to dim each other's brilliance. For example, the complementary color of red is blue-green, and that of green is red; so if red and green are side by side they lend brilliance to each other. If, instead, yellow is put next to red, yellow's blue afterimage makes the red seem purplish, while red's complementary gives the yellow a greenish cast. Chevreul's "law of simultaneous contrasts" pointed out this phenomenon and suggested that to achieve intensity of color it was preferable not to mix pigments on the palette or on the canvas but to keep them separate and allow the colors to combine in the viewer's eye. Further scientific investigations showed that such optical recomposition was best accomplished by using pure pigments in those colors of the spectrum produced when light passes through a prism.

Among these colors, one was conspicuously absent: black, the academic school's favorite. Here then was a scientific theory that answered the young painters' most fervent wishes: the elimination of halftones and the suppression of black. Years later, when Claude Monet died, Georges Clemenceau arrived for a last salute to his friend and saw the coffin bedecked with a black cloth. He pulled it off, tore a multicolored curtain from the window, spread it over the body, and in explanation repeated a saying that he had often heard Monet utter: "Black is not a color." And Clemenceau was entirely correct. Monet and his friends longed for light colors and yearned to make natural light explode on the canvas.

Science, the new rising divinity, urged them: put the sun on your palette. Pissarro had read the physicists' treatises, and the new optical theories had certainly been the object of warm discussions at the Guerbois. Yet direct reliance on science was still unthinkable on the part of artists about 1870. If only nature, rather than the minds of men, could provide them with the magic prism!

Nature did: it gave them the river. Its myriad-faceted surface broke up solid planes into an infinity of reflections that Monet, Pissarro, Renoir and Sisley rendered by means of swiftly applied dapples of almost pure color. The river gave them the means to achieve the miraculous blending of optical theory and freshness of personal vision, of science of color and spontaneity of execution.

And the miracle happened at Argenteuil on the Seine. There the light is so refracted and reflected by the water's prism that the sun's power seems multiplied. Its rays penetrate into all things and creatures, leaving smoldering traces even in their shadows; it dissolves solid forms, blurs clear outlines. Weight and distance explode into a storm of dazzling particles: all is lightness, proximity, immediacy. In picture after picture, the quivering, shimmering surface dazzles our eyes with its exuberance, as when we awaken from sleep on a bright summer morning.

Monet once remarked to a young painter that he would have liked to be born blind and suddenly be granted the gift of sight; these canvases seem to have been painted in just such moments of discovery. The gap between the world and the artist almost vanishes. The intensity of the world's stimuli is matched by the throbbing freshness of the artist's responsiveness; impression and expression have become one. The women with their skirts and hats like blossoms, the sails, the canoeists, are brilliant, passing reflections on the glittering stream of life—a life where everything is a beginning and nothing ends, whence toil and worry are banished; a life reduced to a blissful, eternal Sunday afternoon.

Argenteuil *is* Impressionism. Even when the subjects represented were found in Paris or in Montmartre, the river's enchanted spirit remains evident. So stirring was the vision that revealed itself at Argenteuil to the Batignolles painters that it almost canceled their differences of temperament. Monet and Renoir worked in such harmony that they once were unable to tell their pictures apart. The same technique was employed by all: specks of unmixed pigment were laid down with dizzying speed and sureness and wove themselves into indivisible unity when viewed at a distance. The intense friendship, the solidarity that welded together the members of the group, was precisely the social counterpart of the artistic sharing of what may be called, in every sense of the word, an illumination.

Solidarity was direly needed: light filled the Impressionists' canvases, but in their existence were many grim shadows. Extreme poverty continued to plague them. Practically the only ray of light came from Paul Durand-Ruel, whom Monet and Pissarro had met in London during the war of 1870. Durand-Ruel was the first art dealer in the modern sense. He had inherited an art gallery business from his father, who had known and shown the works of Courbet and the Barbizon painters. Continuing the association with these painters, Durand-Ruel made a

Painting landscapes out of doors—a practice for which the Impressionists were ridiculed no less than for the apparent sloppiness of their work—was not as clumsy an exercise as these cartoons of 1886 suggest. Until the 1840s a *plein air* painter had had to carry his paint in bulky bladders; these, along with easels, canvases and stools, made painting outside the studio a difficult business. Then an American painter named John Rand developed the collapsible, tin paint tube, and painting became portable.

practice of buying their works outright and then reselling them gradually to the public.

His interest in the new generation was aroused by his acquaintance with Monet and Pissarro, and it became active when, in January 1872, he saw Manet's *Moonlight, Harbor at Boulogne* and *Salmon* in the studio of Alfred Stevens. (Such was the spirit of comradeship prevalent among the young artists that, when receiving visits from potential collectors, they displayed their friends' canvases in their own studios.) Durand-Ruel fell in love with Manet's two paintings, went straightaway to see him and purchased them for 1,600 francs. On the following day he returned and bought 23 more, for which he paid 35,000 francs. And a few days later he acquired an additional 16,000 francs' worth.

During the next year or so this new-found benefactor also bought dozens of canvases from Monet, Pissarro, Sisley, Degas and Renoir. He held exhibitions that included their work in London and contributed immeasurably to their material and moral support. At the time, he was able to sell to the public only a very few of his protégés' works, and indeed, his clients began to lose faith in him because of his loyalty to the radical Batignolles artists. But Durand-Ruel stuck to his guns. "A true picture dealer," he wrote, "should also be an enlightened patron. . . . He should, if necessary, sacrifice his immediate interest to his artistic convictions." (His altruism paid off handsomely when Impressionism finally became popular around the 1890s, and his faith in the movement was fully vindicated.)

Unhappily, Durand-Ruel was forced to curtail this enlightened practice temporarily in 1874, when a postwar depression threw him into serious financial difficulties. He ceased buying and the young artists were once again on their own. They seldom sold their pictures, and when they did, so cheaply that it hardly helped. When they ventured to submit their works to the jury of the Salon, the entries were almost automatically rejected. So in 1874, with the determination of a quarry at bay, they chose to defy the enemy—since the Salon did not want them, they would prove to the world that they could conquer the public without the Salon. "The . . . movement no longer needs to fight with others," Degas wrote. "It is, it exists, it has to show itself separately."

Thus the Batignolles artists came up with the idea of formally grouping themselves in an association for the purpose of holding a collective exhibition. Pissarro, in a fit of socialistic fervor, proposed to model it on the cooperative bakers' association of his town of Pontoise. A more practical plan, proposed by Renoir, was accepted: 10 per cent of the income netted by the exhibition was to go into the group's kitty. The core of the membership was provided by the Café Guerbois stalwarts: Monet, Renoir, Sisley, Pissarro, Degas and, in addition, Berthe Morisot.

Degas, who quickly established himself as the association's strategist, convinced his friends that they would stand a better chance if they enlisted other artists. The generous Pissarro readily agreed to the suggestion, which enabled him to invite the younger artists who came to him for guidance: Édouard Béliard, Armand Guillaumin and Cézanne. He experienced some difficulty in having Cézanne accepted by

Degas, who felt that, in order to reassure the public, it would be wise to invite artistically tamer and socially more respectable painters. Some of these, like Tissot and Legros, prudently refused, as did the timorous Fantin-Latour, but more than a dozen from outside the Batignolles regulars accepted, including, at Monet's instigation, their precursor Boudin. So mixed a company would hardly have agreed to any but the most neutral of names; the one finally adopted for the organization was the "Anonymous Cooperative Society of Artists, Sculptors, Engravers, etc. Endowed with Variable Capital and Personnel." A locale was provided by the photographer Nadar, who rented the group a studio he owned at the corner of the Rue Daunou and the Boulevard des Capucines. The exhibition was hung by Renoir—it included 165 works by 30 artists—and opened on April 15, 1874.

If Degas had nourished hopes of diluting the revolutionary character of his own and his friends' entries with the pleasing mediocrity of the other paintings exhibited by the Anonymous Cooperative Society, he was promptly disenchanted. With unerring instinct, the press and public singled out the works of Degas, Monet and their friends; it was the scandal of the Salon des Refusés all over again: indignation, sarcasm, insult rained hard on them. Indeed, little seemed gained by the exhibition save a superb name for the movement. Auguste Renoir's brother, Edmond, who was in charge of the catalogue, had complained to Monet about the monotony of his titles. To please him, Monet pointed to a canvas and, probably recalling a term that frequently came up in the discussions at the Guerbois, said: "Call it *Impression, Sunrise" (page 118)*. A reporter spied this title and, in what he intended as derogatory sarcasm, dubbed Monet and his friends "Impressionists." So fitting was the term that it was soon adopted, not only by their opponents, but by the artists themselves.

When the Impressionists held their fourth show in 1879, critics continued to ridicule the artists' loose style and color-splashed canvases. This cartoon from the periodical *Le Charivari* pressed the attack, humorously suggesting insanity as the most charitable explanation for their unconventional techniques. The caption read: "New School of Independent Painting. Independent of their will, we hope for their sake."

For more than a decade the Impressionists continued to show their works as a group, but inevitably the diversity of their personalities and backgrounds began to split them apart. Their solidarity, born of comradeship, bolstered by hardship and immortalized in a name, gradually dissolved until, by the time the eighth and last Impressionist exhibition was held, in 1886, the group had practically ceased to exist. The erstwhile comrades were engaged, according to one of their later admirers, Van Gogh, in "disastrous civil wars," and he added: "On all sides, they try to play nasty tricks on each other with a zeal worthy of a better cause." In 1880 Monet replied to a journalist who asked him whether he had ceased to consider himself an Impressionist, "Not at all, I still am, and I always intend to be an Impressionist . . . but now I meet my colleagues, men and women, only very rarely. The little church has today become a banal school that opens its doors to any dauber." The miracle was a thing of the past.

It had begun with Monet's arrival in Argenteuil in 1872; it ended with his departure, in 1878, when he settled at Vétheuil, again on the Seine but farther downstream. The incomparably graceful, carefree Sunday of painting had lasted six years. Now the delicate balance of youthful, unselfconscious Impressionism was broken. The Impressionists had caught the fugitive instant by responding to it with the freshness of what they called *la sensation première*—"the first sensation." Now the freshness, the firstness was disappearing. To compensate for this loss, they relied more than before on theory; intuition gave way to system, experience to experiment. Even the gentle, undoctrinaire Sisley succumbed: the later landscapes that he painted at Moret-sur-Loing—where he was to die of cancer, poor, untalked about, in 1899—were built on the same pattern as before, but they became harsh, brittle and almost devoid of the subtlety and sensitivity of old.

In Monet, too, opportunity hardened into a kind of code though he never abandoned Impressionism. In his serial paintings of haystacks and cathedrals *(page 117)*—setting up several easels in a studio opposite Rouen cathedral, he painted a succession of pictures of the building's façade, striving to catch in each the different color effects of light created at a different time of day—he tried to give his eye the infallible precision of an optical instrument. As he probed further and further, with obsessional perseverance, into the constitution of those inseparable intangibles, time and light, his experiments finally led him, in the luminous whirls of his water-lily paintings *(pages 120-121)*, to a near-abstract grandeur. Year after year he was to treat this theme in his garden at Giverny, his last home, where he died in 1926.

The fascination with experiment that led Monet toward abstraction took other painters into less fertile fields. The optical exploration of the Impressionists had been guided in a general way by scientific principles; two young artists, Georges Seurat and Paul Signac, decided around 1884 that strict doctrine and rigorously conducted experiment had to take the place of improvisation. The result was Pointillism, a pseudo-scientific style to which Seurat and Signac succeeded in converting the dean of Impressionism, Pissarro *(page 117)*. Pointillism carried the color theories of Impressionism into the realm of dogma; tiny points of pigment were applied in regulated color combinations to form stiff, tapestrylike and often charming paintings. For about four years, Pissarro lined up his *petits points* with touching zeal—but at last he could no longer bear the tedium of Pointillism, and from around 1890 to his death in 1903 he again painted landscapes that recapture some of the freedom and freshness of his Impressionistic phase.

Pissarro's disciple Cézanne was also discontented with the fluidity of Impressionism and likewise eager to build on stabler ground: rather than in optical science, however, he sought it in the permanent, geometric structure of earth—a long, strenuous pursuit that culminated in a series of powerful pictures of Mont Sainte-Victoire, near Aix-en-Provence, where Cézanne lived, worked and died, a lone wolf, in 1906.

Renoir, like his friends, felt the need to rely on something stable to make up for lost natural ebullience. Turning away from the shimmering fabric of Impressionism, Renoir cultivated a closed form using a tight, neat line. The result, as in Sisley's later works, tended to be morose and dry. It was no longer fun and, in Renoir's case, what was not fun was not good. Fortunately, his irrepressible nature soon reacted against system, and after several years of self-inflicted seriousness, Renoir

Renoir loved to paint and draw beautiful women all his life. The drawing above was made when he was 50. At 66, he turned to sculpture, but within a few years his hands had become so crippled by rheumatism that he was unable to execute his ideas himself. *The Washerwoman (below)* is one of more than 30 pieces of sculpture made by a young Spaniard named Richard Guino to whom Renoir communicated his design with sketches, words and, occasionally, a sweeping gesture of his crippled hands.

reverted to his true nature. "I am struggling with blossoming trees, with women and children, and I don't want to see anything beyond that," he wrote in 1881. The reward was a second youth that was to last until his death in 1919. Despite the painful rheumatism that crippled him in his later years—he had to have the brush tied to his gnarled, petrified hand—his work was a joyous ode to life, a blazing hymn to the force that blossomed in plant, woman and child.

And Manet? By painting side by side with Monet and Renoir in Argenteuil and by helping Monet to find a house there, he had had a hand in the miracle. His friendship for Monet never slackened. Time and again he responded to his pleas for financial help. At one particularly critical time, he asked Duret to assist the destitute and despondent "Raphael of water," as he called Monet, by purchasing a number of canvases; and the delicacy of his feelings made him invent a stratagem whereby Monet would be led to believe that the purchase had been made by a dealer.

Yet when the Batignolles "gang" invited their leader to exhibit with them in 1874, he refused. No amount of entreaty by Monet, Degas or even Berthe Morisot succeeded in making him change his mind. Neither then nor in any of the association's subsequent exhibitions did Manet exhibit with the Impressionists.

Why this refusal? Because Manet had had his fill of scandal. More than 10 years had elapsed since the uproar of *Luncheon on the Grass*, 10 years of abuse. More than ever, Manet yearned for official recognition. "I shall never exhibit in the stand next door; I shall enter the Salon by the main door," he told Duranty. Shortly before the Impressionist exhibit this old hope seemed at last on the verge of coming true. In 1873, his picture *Le Bon Bock* had not only been accepted by the Salon but achieved popular success—so much that an actor in a local theater re-enacted Manet's replete, jovial beer-drinker in a *tableau vivant*. The success was due to the reassuringly traditional look of the picture, done in the long-accepted genre manner of the Haarlem painter, Frans Hals. (When a critic jokingly remarked, "Manet has put water in his wine," Alfred Stevens sarcastically added, "Not water; Haarlem beer.")

Now, just at the moment when it seemed to Manet that the bourgeois public was about to forgive his scandalous past, his young friends wanted him to plunge back into the nightmare! Manet would not have it.

There were also more subtle reasons for his refusal. He did not feel that his aims coincided with those of Impressionism. To be sure, he had allowed his friends' contagious enthusiasm to sweep him out of the studio into the sun-drenched *plein air*, to the riverbank of Argenteuil and its whirl of luminous reflections. The instant, shimmering texture of Sunday on the Seine finds glorious expression in such pictures as *Monet in His Studio Boat (page 115)* and *Argenteuil (page 113)*. *Blue Venice* is a dazzling splurge of refracted sun-play. And nowhere perhaps has the impact of momentary sensation received fresher rendering than in Manet's picture of Monet painting in his garden or in *Rue Mosnier Decked with Flags (page 146)*. In these works, Manet even gave up the solid massing and firm outlining that characterized him and adopted the Impressionists' technique. The brush darts to and fro, nervous strokes of color pelt the canvas in almost anarchic profusion.

Yet Manet had never really been converted to Impressionism. Closer inspection reveals that he did not model his palette on the colors of the prism; nor did he banish black from his canvas. Rather than conform to Impressionist theory and practice, he had taken from them what suited his own pursuit: freedom, the constant struggle against routine. For a short while—as long as the improvisatory freshness that blossomed at Argenteuil lasted—Manet went along with Monet and his friends. But as they increasingly resorted to method, Manet instinctively refused to follow. For him there could be no method, no scientific truth, no foolproof style: "Every time I paint, I throw myself into the water in order to learn how to swim."

The Impressionists were unable to sustain for long this heroic rejection of tested knowledge. Instead, they fell back on the very tenet on which traditional art had been based since the Renaissance—that painting was, first and foremost, a matter of seeing. They questioned it no more than had Courbet; they merely claimed that they saw better, thanks to the help of scientific method. Similarly, the Pointillists who followed them—Seurat, Signac—were to assert that *they* saw still better, that they were to the Impressionists what scientific research was to prescientific groping.

Manet continued to affirm, as he had since the early '60s, that painting was a matter not of sight, but of insight, that the act of painting could not be confused with the act of seeing. To confuse them was to subordinate painting to seeing, which condemned painting to be derivative, secondhand, past; whereas Manet could not allow anything to be more important than the act of painting. A truthful representation of subject matter was possible only when the paint used to delineate it was as vital to the picture as the image itself. Paint was paint. It had a reality of its own over and above the image it reproduced. This was the real revolution brought about by Manet, and on that ground he remained alone and misunderstood, even by his admirers. Their opinion is summarized by the art critic and novelist J. K. Huysmans: "He indicated the road but he himself remained stationary. . . . In sum, M. Manet is today outstripped by most of the painters who in the past considered him, rightly, as a master." Indeed, this opinion, based on a misguided notion of artistic progress, still crops up today, and it is not unusual to hear specialists assert that Manet's later work is feeble in comparison to that of the '60s.

Manet himself would have been hard put to plead his case. There were as yet no words to explain, no painters to corroborate with their work the tremendous upheaval he had caused. All he could say, to dissociate himself from the reversion of his friends to the old, familiar pattern, was: "I paint as I feel like painting; to hell with all their studies." And he added: "An artist has to be a spontaneist." Impressionism, for Monet and his colleagues, had been a final choice; they settled in its doctrine as one settles in the country. For Manet, the country was merely a place where you spent your summer holiday.

A Blaze of Color

The most popular paintings in the world today are those of the Impressionists. An original Impressionist canvas can command hundreds of thousands of dollars—although they were sold in their time for a pittance—and as reproductions they have found their way into millions of homes. And yet the enormous impact on public taste generated by Impressionism was achieved by a handful of artists in a very short time. Barely a dozen years elapsed between the first group exhibition of Impressionists in 1874, and the last, in 1886. But even before then the movement was dissipating. Among the leaders, who included Claude Monet, Camille Pissarro and Pierre-Auguste Renoir, only Alfred Sisley continued throughout his career to paint in the original style.

Manet was a great friend of the Impressionists. He inspired them with his own rebellious example and even briefly experimented with their techniques, as the sunstruck boating scene at the right shows. But he chose not to exhibit with them and never considered himself an Impressionist.

Perhaps the greatest single figure in Impressionism was Monet, whose painting *Impression, Sunrise (page 118)* lent the movement its name. Along with his good friend Renoir, the older Pissarro, the dedicated Sisley and a few other gifted men, Monet sought to capture the elusive effects of light in nature, and in doing so, created a shimmering legacy of beautiful and enduring paintings.

"Suddenly, without warning, he flashed a magnesium lamp in our faces and all but blinded us," wrote one critic about the stunning effect of Manet's Argenteuil riverscapes. Under the influence of his friends he had adopted a new and brighter palette. The holiday atmosphere of the place added its own gaiety to this picture. Still, though, the Salon critics scoffed ("the indigo river is as flat as a wall"), and Manet's bright, spontaneous technique seemed nothing more than "a wretched daub."

Argenteuil, 1874

If any place can be considered the home of Impressionism it is Argenteuil. Now an industrial suburb, Argenteuil in the 1870s was a haven of country comforts, regattas on the Seine and lush cottage gardens. Monet's view of the bridge and catboats above captures the bright, hot noontime stillness of the place.

In 1874 Argenteuil became less a resort than a refuge. The first Impressionist exhibition that spring had been a disaster, critically and financially. Monet fled to Argenteuil, where he had previously rented a house, but

Manet, *Monet in His Studio Boat*, 1874

Monet, *The Bridge at Argenteuil*, 1874

Renoir, *Monet Painting in His Garden*, 1873

his landlord threatened to evict him—probably over the rent. Manet responded generously by finding him another place, where he was soon joined by Renoir. Exchanging ideas, painting the same scenes, the friends often worked side-by-side and even used each other as models. Renoir painted Monet in his garden; Manet showed Monet and his wife in the floating studio that he had built to get nearer to his watery subjects. Painting was the summer's food; the dazzling light on the river, the flower colors, would nourish these artists for many years.

115

The evolution of Impressionism

Claude Monet

More than any other Impressionist Monet sought to trap the fleeting sensation of light in nature. Gradually, in his work, solid forms disappeared, until even the façade of Rouen Cathedral (*second from right*) seems eroded by the blazing sun. At the end of his life he was still studying reflections in a pond (*far right*).

1866-1867

1869

1875-1878

Renoir

If the second painting from the left resembles the one above it, the reason is that Renoir and Monet painted the scene side by side, as they often did during their early friendship. But Renoir's interest in picturing the ripe glow of womanhood led him away from landscapes and to paeans of praise to beauty.

1867

c. 1869

c. 1875

C. Pissarro

Born 10 years earlier than Monet and Renoir, Pissarro was one of the first to experiment with the techniques of Impressionism and among the last to abandon them. But he dallied briefly with Pointillism in paintings like the one second from the right, which vibrates with dots of pure primary colors.

c. 1864

1870

1872

Sisley

More of a follower than an innovator, Sisley found the goals of Impressionism perfectly suited to him. And among the pictures that he painted between 1872 and 1876—the zenith of the style—are some of its masterworks. His snow scenes (*third from left*) in particular are unrivaled in delicacy.

1866

1874

For the titles and collection credits of these paintings, see page 187.

1877   1884

1905   late

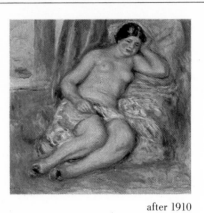

1883   1884-1887   1890   after 1910

1874   1878   1888   1898

1878   1888   1892   1893

Claude Monet

Born in Paris and raised by the sea at Le Havre, Monet had a lifelong love affair with water, light, air and color. He aimed, as one critic put it, "to reveal no more of reality than the shifting flux of appearances." True to this aim, on one flag-decked national holiday in Paris, as he was walking along the street with his painting equipment, he spied a balcony above the street from which he thought an interesting view could be had, climbed the stairs, asked and got permission and painted the picture at the right. Similarly, it is the exact instant that the morning sun burns through the mist of Le Havre harbor that occupied Monet in the painting below, from which Impressionism took its name.

Monet, *Self-portrait*, 1917

Monet, *Impression, Sunrise*, 1872

Monet, *Rue Montorgueil Decked with Flags*, 1878

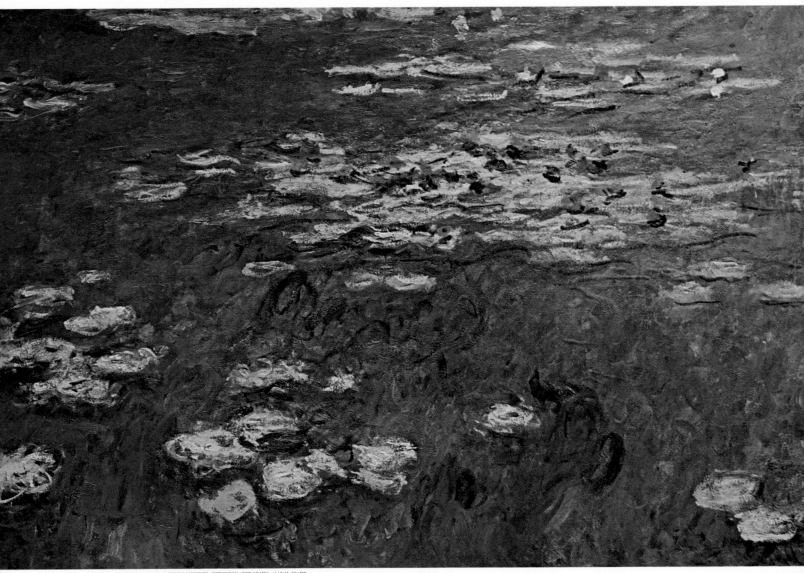

More than anything else it was water that fascinated Monet throughout his life. An enthusiastic sailor (the floating studio he had had constructed at Argenteuil was large enough for him to sleep in and to use for trips with his family up and down the river), he was never far from a river or the ocean during his long life. Finally, he even created his own private piece of water. In 1890, when he was 50, Monet bought a farmhouse in the quiet, rolling countryside near Giverny, midway between Paris and Le Havre. There, by diverting a tiny river, he built a water

Monet, *Nymphéas (Water Lilies)*, 1920-1926

garden that became the subject of most of the important paintings of his later years.

Before he died, in 1926 at the age of 86, Monet had painted scores of pictures of his watery, plant-filled garden. Some he destroyed, for he was a ferocious critic of his own work. For 36 years Monet wrestled with this one subject and, seeking to involve the viewer more fully in his scenes, he created larger and larger pictures. The one above, painted when his eyesight was failing, is almost 20 feet across—an environment in itself.

Renoir

Renoir, *Self-portrait*, 1875

Renoir first met his future colleagues Monet and Sisley in Paris in 1862. For the next 20 years the three artists worked together to hammer out the pure-color, light-defining esthetic of Impressionism. In the 1880s, however, Renoir paused: "I was coming to the conclusion that I did not know either how to paint or draw." And while the dazzling picture at the right seems to belie Renoir's self-criticism, it shows that he was already moving away from typically Impressionist outdoor subjects and that his painting style was changing to include a concern for form and volume as much as with light and color. In the end, the human figure, especially beautiful women like the model Nini Lopez shown here, preoccupied him.

Renoir, *The Seine at Asnières*, 1878

Renoir, *The Loge*, 1874

Capturing the gaiety of a summer outing, Renoir painted a group of his handsome young friends as they sat after lunch at a *guingette*, or country tavern, following an excursion on the Seine, probably at or near Argenteuil. The girl playing with the dog is Aline Charigot, a favorite model of Renoir's; she became his wife soon after this picture was finished. Also at the table is Angèle, another favorite model, who enjoyed what was politely described as a "colorful reputation."

One of the most interesting figures in the picture is the young man straddling the chair in the right foreground. He is Gustave Caillebotte, a wealthy naval architect who was also a talented dilettante painter and an important early collector of Impressionist works. It was Caillebotte who helped Monet outfit his floating studio and thus met Renoir, Sisley and the others. Delighted to find himself among a group of such talented, articulate professionals, Caillebotte bought their works both to help them out and because he liked the pictures. While still in his twenties, Caillebotte wrote a will that left his entire collection to the French people. But at his death, only 18 years later in 1894, such a furor arose over accepting these still-daring paintings ("For the government to accept such filth, there would have to be a great moral slackening," wrote one academic painter) that only 38 of the 67 offered works were taken. The rest were sold. Today, many paintings from Caillebotte's collection grace the Jeu de Paume Museum, the sunny treasure-house of Impressionist masterpieces near the Louvre in the Tuileries Garden in Paris.

Renoir, *Luncheon of the Boating Party*, 1881

C. Pissarro

Peering over his half-rim glasses, Camille Pissarro *(left)* at the age of 68 looks every bit the wry, good-humored patriarch of art. Until he died at 73, he never slackened in his enthusiasm for laying paint on canvas nor lost the unflagging kindness that made him friend and mentor to many younger artists. Born at St. Thomas in the West Indies, Pissarro became convinced on an early trip to Paris that he wanted to paint, and returned at 25 to make his way in art. All his life he sought to capture the many-dimensioned reality of a place and as these three paintings show, he was able to render precisely the look of weather, the feel of atmosphere and the sense of time of year.

Pissarro, *Self-portrait*, 1898

Pissarro, *A Gray Day on the Banks of the Oise, near Pontoise*, 1878

Pissarro, *Carriage at Louveciennes*, 1874

Pissarro, *Boulevard Montmartre, Spring*, 1897

In 1877, Pissarro painted 53 pictures, more than one a week. It was not unusual for the Impressionists to work this quickly. They were, after all, painting directly from nature and they aimed at catching the physical qualities of the scene before them just as they saw it. Obviously, if they could not do this quickly, they could not do it at all. But Pissarro's amazing rate of work indicates an unusual degree of control of hand and eye, and the supreme self-confidence of the 47-year-old Pissarro, then at the height of his powers, is manifest in the landscape at the right. It is much more than a quick slapdash of formless bright colors. Indeed, one of the characteristics of almost all of Pissarro's paintings is that he manages, as he does here, to convey a convincing sense of depth in the scene. He also, as usual, has chosen his point of view with great care —although it seems quite casual—so that his painting appears solidly composed and yet is neither formal, nor quaintly "picturesque." This sense of structure and mass is especially clear in the sharp angles and planes of the village roofs and in the placement of the trees.

One of the perceptive appreciators of painting in the Impressionist period, Théodore Duret, summed up Pissarro best: "You have neither Sisley's decorative flair nor Monet's fantastic eye, but you have what they lack, a deep, intimate feeling for nature that makes a fine canvas by you absolutely four-square and sound."

Pissarro, *The Red Roofs, Edge of a Village, in Winter*, 1877

129

Renoir, *Portrait of Sisley*, 1875-1876

Sisley

Alfred Sisley lived a life of extreme and unremitting poverty and relentless dedication to the Impressionist ideal. Here, he has taken what might have been a tragic subject—a tiny village inundated by a flooding river—and made of it a scene as full of sunlit charm as a Renoir boating picture. Typically, it is not the drama of the flood that interests Sisley but the play of light on the risen water, the reflections on the building façade, and the stark, feathery trees standing like ghosts of the day. The decorative flair with which Duret credited Sisley in his remark to Pissarro is evident in the wonderful pattern of bright color that fills the picture from edge to edge.

Sisley never earned more than a few hundred francs for a picture. Ironically, a few months after his death, another painting that Sisley had made of this same scene was auctioned for 45,150 francs.

Sisley, *The Flood at Port Marly*, 1876

VI

Their Subject Was Paris

Fascinated by the railroad as a symbol of the pace and power of the industrial era, Manet painted this indirect portrait of a steamy engine as it whistles its way toward a Parisian railway station. Juxtaposed against the unseen iron beast is the soft innocence of a woman and child, the little girl fascinated by the clattery scene below. The girl was the daughter of a fellow artist, the woman was the artist's model, Victorine Meurend, who had posed for *Olympia* and *Luncheon on the Grass.*

The Railway (Gare Saint-Lazare), 1873

"I think only of returning to Paris," Manet once wrote to his friend Fantin-Latour from Boulogne, where he was vacationing, "for I do nothing here. Two months is decidedly too long." A Parisian to the marrow, Manet needed the excitement of the city. He preferred the reflections of chandeliers in mirrors to those of the sun on water; he gladly traded fields and glades for plants in a hothouse; and when it came to representing the well-known hunter and African explorer, Pertuiset, he casually substituted a hide for a live lion and a Montmartre garden for the jungle of Africa.

It was a gay, busy, throbbing Paris that Manet knew in the '70s. Despite the colossal indemnity imposed on the new Third Republic after the defeat suffered in the Franco-Prussian War, France recovered with breathtaking swiftness. The process of conversion from a preindustrial, semiprovincial capital into a modern megalopolis, inaugurated under Napoleon III, continued. In 1861, 70 per cent of France's population was rural; 20 years later, the percentage had dropped to 65 per cent. In street after street, standardized apartment buildings of the kind introduced by Baron Haussmann were going up. Industry and the proletariat grew apace: the near future held the promise of material progress and the threat of social crisis.

For the moment, it was the happier aspect of city life that prevailed—or that bourgeois liberals like Manet chose to see. And there was much for the insouciant Parisian *boulevardier* to look at. The high spots of fashion had not changed: Longchamp, the Bois, the Café de Bade, Café Tortoni still exerted their magnetic attraction. In 1875, Paris' social life found a new center: the new Opéra, the biggest and most lavish in the world, begun in 1862 under Napoleon III by the architect Charles Garnier (who also designed the Monte Carlo casino) and inaugurated at long last by the Third Republic's President Mac-Mahon. "Must we admit that the center of this powerful city is today an opera house?" the austere newspaper *Le Temps* lamented. "Are we no longer anything more than the capital of elegance and leisure?"

Another temple of a different sort of art, opened just before the Sec-

The first successful bicycle with rotary cranks, known then as a velocipede, was reputedly built in Paris in 1865. Bicycling quickly became one of high society's favorite pastimes. Even women enjoyed the sport, especially after a fashionable doctor declared the exercise to be beneficial. The ladies apparently were undaunted by the clumsiness of their vast crinoline skirts *(below)*, which at the peak of their fashion in the 1860s were sometimes as wide as the wearer was tall. The bicycle went on to even greater vogue in the following decades, but after the war of 1870 the crinoline disappeared from Paris streets— to be replaced by the bustle.

ond Empire collapsed, now came into its own: the Folies-Bergère. It is hard to say whether its success was due to its variety shows or to its *promenoir*—the aisle behind the orchestra seats, paced by demimondaines of whom the manager required only one thing: that they be sumptuously attired. The same ladies of pleasure also displayed their charms at the *café-concerts*, where the customers ate and drank while singers performed; or at the skating rinks—a new fad—and of course at the Longchamp race track, where they were restricted to the infield (so that one might distinguish them from the real ladies, the wits said). The combined pressures of middle-class puritanism and working-class poverty made this the last great age of courtesanry. Manet's eye followed these ladies with obvious relish. And not just his eye. One day his plumpish wife saw him following a slim girl in the street. "I caught you this time," she laughingly said to him. Unruffled, he replied: "Oh, I thought it was you."

In many ways the city offered an altered face to the curious onlooker. Haussmann's grand design for the reconstruction of Paris was being carried forward by the Third Republic, and the city was now laced by wide, tree-lined avenues. The streets, both old and new, were filled with horse-cabs driven by redoubtable tyrants in thick cloaks and battered leather hats. With luck, contemporary observers noted, you might convince one of them to take you to your destination for the standard fee of one and a half francs, if, of course, he were going your way. The horse-drawn omnibuses were cheaper but more crowded. Many a romance, if we are to believe the novels of the time, started on the upper deck, known as the *impériale*. Bicycles had appeared in the streets; men were beginning to sport side whiskers instead of beards; women, repudiating the crinoline, had deflated their skirts.

Manet absorbed the spectacle of the city with undiminished avidity. Unlike Paris, he had not changed; on the threshold of middle age, he was as exuberant, flippant and sociable as ever. If anything, success provided his thirst for worldly pleasures with new and richer satisfactions. For success was at last coming his way. *Le Bon Bock* had been one of the hits of the Salon of 1873. Manet was no longer so dependent on family wealth and could now rely on the support of his dealer, Durand-Ruel, and of a handful of collectors such as the celebrated baritone Jean-Baptiste Faure. In 1871 he had moved from his studio on the Rue Guyot in the Batignolles quarter to one on Rue de Saint-Pétersbourg, in the chic Europe district. Now he moved again, to a larger, more handsome studio on the same street. And on his letterhead he exultantly inscribed: *Tout arrive*, "Everything happens."

Everything" was an overstatement. Manet's success was both sporadic and ambiguous. At the Salon of 1873, *Le Bon Bock* pleased the conservative public, but *Resting*, a boldly handled portrait of Berthe Morisot, shocked them. In 1876, one of the members of the jury that turned down *The Laundress* snapped: "That's enough. We have given M. Manet ten years to amend himself. He hasn't done so. On the contrary, he is sinking deeper. *Refusé!*" Even favorable critics, such as Théophile Silvestre, considered Manet a case of arrested development:

"Manet in some respects is an interesting artist, but an embryonic artist." One of the chief complaints against him was that he did not finish his pictures. The hands—they said—were especially raw (how one understands Manet's elation when Antonin Proust begged him not to add another stroke to the gloves of his portrait!). After 1870, Manet's manner of painting, with its flurries of free-wheeling, visible brushstrokes, was even less compatible than his earlier one with the qualities of "finish" on which the conservatives insisted.

With Manet, in fact, *succès de scandale* seemed to go hand in hand with *succès d'estime*. After the insulting refusal by the jury in 1876 of *The Laundress* and a portrait of Marcellin Desboutin called *The Artist*, Manet decided to exhibit the ostracized pictures in his studio. Four thousand people passed through it between April 15 and May 1. The show attracted considerable critical praise but also the usual scoffers. So thick was the crowd, so noisy were the discussions that the neighbors complained; the landlord later refused Manet's request to renew his lease.

Manet himself sometimes chose to ignore the differences between esteem and scandal, for his eagerness to achieve fame was greater than ever. Degas was right in calling his friend a bourgeois: Manet would have painted more acceptable pictures had he been able to do so. Some, like *In the Conservatory* or *Woman in Evening Dress*, are indeed on the borderline of conventional art. He said kind things about the work of the fashionable portraitist Chaplin and he was fascinated by Carolus-Duran, a shallow virtuoso of the brush whose glib adaptation of Velázquez' style earned him prices 20 times as high as those obtained by Manet. The two became friends; they even began portraits of each other, but neither portrait was finished, Manet getting no further than a theatrical sketch of the subject in riding clothes. "We exchanged two shots but failed to hit," Manet commented jokingly. The episode may stand as a symbol for Manet's unsuccessful flirtation with Salon art.

Against such disappointments, Manet's favorite antidote was crowds of people milling about him, chatting and laughing. He loved dinners, parties and balls. He enjoyed the distinguished musical soirees that his wife gave regularly on Tuesdays. His own studio filled, after five o'clock, with friends, acquaintances, ladies of *le monde* and of *le demi-monde*, and journalists on the lookout for anecdotes. His wife aptly described it as "an annex of the Café de Bade." Beer and apéritifs were, in fact, set out on a table.

These sociable gatherings attracted a sophisticated and often notable company. There could be seen the subtle Symbolist poet Stéphane Mallarmé, who had taken the late Baudelaire's place in the artist's affections (Baudelaire had died, half insane, in 1867). Manet had Mallarmé sit for one of his finest portraits and he illustrated the poet's *Afternoon of a Faun* with several wood engravings; he also embellished Mallarmé's translation of Edgar Allan Poe's *The Raven* with a superb series of lithographs that proved his feeling for dramatic black-and-white contrasts to be as sharp as during his Spanish period. Another poet friend was Charles Cros, who added to his talent for verse (some of

Among the several books that Manet illustrated for friends was Stéphane Mallarmé's translation of Edgar Allan Poe's *The Raven*. In 1874 he made the lithograph above for the text of the poem and the drawing of the raven's head at top for a poster that advertised the book. The Manet-Mallarmé collaboration was first published in a limited edition of 240 copies signed by both artists.

which Manet illustrated) a gift for technical discoveries: he discovered the principle of the phonograph before Edison.

Cros introduced Manet to his mistress Nina de Callias, who called herself de Villard after she left her journalist husband. An eccentric but warm-hearted nymphomaniac, she threw her arms and her house wide open to avant-garde writers, artists and musicians. Drink and talk flowed in profusion at her flat until the early hours of the morning. Manet has left us a striking portrait of the aging beauty in *The Woman with the Fans*.

Manet's friendship with another lady of easy virtue, Méry Laurent, is believed to have been more intimate. While still very young, she had run away from her husband, a grocer in Nancy, to become a nude dancer on a Paris stage—the ideal platform for launching oneself in the career of love. She had become the mistress of one of Napoleon III's generals, Canrobert, and afterwards of Dr. Thomas W. Evans, a United States citizen who became the Emperor's personal dentist. While Evans kept her—most generously, it should be said—she gave herself to artists and writers. Mallarmé was her close friend and Manet soon came to appreciate her intelligence, charm and taste. An exquisite late portrait bears witness to their tender friendship.

To another of Manet's favorite models, Victorine Meurend, the world was not so kind. Manet had accosted her in the street in 1862. Her agitated love life—perhaps not altogether unblemished by venality—eventually took her to America. After her return, around 1873, she again posed for Manet. In time, her contact with the artist aroused artistic ambitions in her and she took up painting and even managed to exhibit several times at the Salon. But Manet's talent had not communicated itself to her. She fell into poverty, drank more and more, and finally the lovely model of so many illustrious pictures, from *The Street Singer* to *The Railway (Gare St.-Lazare) (page 132)*, disappeared from the records of history.

Portraits were the natural product of Manet's crowded life, and he produced dozens of them. There were portraits of celebrities, such as the politician Clemenceau, of friends, of women; portraits done in oil and also in pastels, a technique he increasingly utilized after 1873, for it allowed him the widest range of effects, from the velvety softness of *Madame Manet* to the slashing brutality of *George Moore (slipcase)*. The portraits echo the mosaic of faces with which the painter liked to surround himself, even while he worked. "One must either be one of a thousand or all alone," Manet professed. Afraid of being alone, he tried to be one of a thousand.

But the social crowd merely covered up his artistic solitude. The conservatives still feared him as the leader of the revolutionaries, while many in the Impressionist generation regarded him as a timid, outstripped precursor. Manet's gang had transferred its headquarters from the Guerbois to a café on the Place Pigalle, La Nouvelle Athènes, but the group had diminished. Monet, Pissarro and Cézanne dropped in there, but they were too caught up with the countryside to do so more than occasionally. Renoir continued to live in Paris, but he joined his former comrades only infrequently. Of the old Guerbois group, only one regular remained, but his artistic authority had been growing steadily, so much so in fact that his influence had exerted itself even on Manet: Edgar Degas.

Degas was even more allergic to the countryside than was Manet. "If I were the government," he quipped, "I'd have the police watch landscapists." He refused to be called an Impressionist. That term was good for the likes of Monet and Pissarro, who roamed the fields; Degas' preference went to closed rooms and to artificial lighting. He chose the city over the country and the products of human industry over the fruits of nature. "A painting is an artificial work existing outside nature," he once explained, "and it requires as much cunning as the perpetration of a crime." Nothing could be more artificial than the world of ballet and it was in this world that he had already begun to immerse himself.

Ballet scenes had first appeared in Degas' work in 1868. But before Degas could exploit ballet themes, the Franco-Prussian War interrupted his development. After the war, in 1872, he took a trip to New Orleans to visit an uncle and two brothers, who were cotton merchants. The time of his return from America coincides with the first flowering of his mature style. It also marks the beginning of a physical difficulty that would aggravate his neurotic tendency to be a solitary misanthrope. His eyes, which he claimed had been weakened by the long, cold nights he spent in an unheated studio during the siege of Paris, began to give him trouble that would get progressively worse for the rest of his life. The death of his father, followed in 1875 by the failure of the New Orleans family business, transformed Degas from affluent bourgeois into penurious artist. (He relinquished his part of the paternal inheritance and even sold his valuable collection of old masters to help his brothers pay their debts and thereby spare the respectable name of Degas from being blemished.)

Henceforth, he depended for a living on the sale of his works to Durand-Ruel and to collectors, to him an agonizing dependency, for he not only disliked turning an avocation—passionate though his attachment to it was—into a profession, but he also found it torture to part with paintings which, he felt, had not yet attained flawless perfection. More than once, in fact, he failed to deliver a promised picture or sought to recover it from its owner in order to improve upon it.

Perfection to Degas was not a gift of the gods, but the result of study, perseverance, training and control—like the ballerina's dance. "Nothing in art must look like an accident—not even motion." Hence Degas' preference for subjects with codified, predictable gestures and movements: dancers drilled by ballet masters, horses responding to jockeys' orders, milliners or laundresses endlessly repeating their laborious routines. Painters until now had looked at life as it happened: Degas tried to make it a controlled experiment.

This was the very time when the writings of scientists like the physiologist Claude Bernard or the chemist Pierre-Eugène Berthelot stimulated not only experimental research but also the minds of artists and writers. Émile Zola found in experimental doctrine the theoretical framework for his so-called Naturalist novels. Naturalism, as he saw it, was to its precursor, Realism, what proved theories are to experimental discoveries. The sharply observed characters in the Realistic novels of Gustave Flaubert, almost 20 years Zola's senior, remained people; Zola's characters became guinea pigs. Faithful description yielded to what Zola fancied to be scientific documentation. To him the life of individuals was the predictable consequence of a series of testable factors, above all, heredity. He, like Degas, saw in the city and industrial society a cultural milieu more easily analyzed than nature and rural existence, and therefore more suitable to what he might have called, as Degas did, his "art calculations."

Zola's scientific system was hardly more than pseudoscience, a stretched-out metaphor borrowed from developing theories in natural science (and fortunately redeemed by his bursts of truly epic power); but in Degas' case the word "calculations" is not too strong. He measured his models with calipers. Perfection for him was "the right, right moment," that is to say, the very pinpoint perfection that enables a good ballerina to defeat temporarily the leaden pull of gravity.

This precision is, for Degas, an absolute necessity. Like a dancer, a picture, pushed and pulled by contradictory forces, will collapse unless it disposes itself dynamically around its center of gravity. But whereas a living body finds its point of equilibrium by natural, instinctive adjustment, Degas in his pictures arrived at it by conscious investigation. Contradictory, unbalancing forces had tugged at Degas' art from the outset. As a young man he acknowledged these conflicting attractions toward both classical tradition and contemporary reality when he wrote in a notebook, "Ah, Giotto, let me see Paris, and you, Paris, let me see Giotto." Actually, he was determined to have the nobility of Giotto and the reality of Paris, just as, on another plane, he was able to worship Ingres and also admire Delacroix.

Nothing illustrates the tensions under which Degas labored more strikingly than his ballet scenes *(pages 158-161)*. The contrast between stage dream and backstage reality is artfully emphasized. The graceful youth of the butterfly-hued dancers clashes with the hoariness of the ballet master or the rich old "protectors" dressed in black, waiting behind a set for their delicate prey to leave the limelight. The girls' fairy elegance itself is contradicted by their native gawkiness and torpor, which re-emerge the moment they are no longer performing—queens in the detail-dimming distance and illumination of the stage, mere concierges' daughters in the stark close-up of the dressing room.

In these pictures, an idealist and a cynic are locked in deadly battle. On them is projected the excruciating predicament of a Degas torn—like Manet—between his respect for the past and his fascination with the present. His colors often have an old-masterly darkness; the modeling of his figures is sometimes of the most traditional and conventional sort (Degas once said he wished he had the "execution of a Bouguereau," who was the very symbol of academic art); and he wanted his pictures to convey a considerable mass of direct information about the figures in them. For these reasons he remained loyal to the three-dimensional space elaborated by the Renaissance. Indeed, in order to make linear perspective more powerful he accentuated it by making the oblique lines that define it daringly steep (an effect he achieved by choosing unusually high, low or close points of view).

On the other hand, Degas cherished at least as much as Manet the modern concern with the two-dimensionality of painting. His compositions, strongly influenced by Japanese woodcuts, stress surface patterns. As in Manet's *Olympia*, heavy outlines turn three-dimensional forms into two-dimensional designs. Thus two systems of lines are at work in Degas' paintings: the one, based on diagonals, relating the figures to the distant, imaginary background; the other, based on surface patterns, pressing them forward to the picture plane.

This perpetual tug-of-war explains Degas' passionate striving for "the right, right moment." There is one point where the conflict between the system of lines creating deep space and the pattern lines of the surface is temporarily resolved, a point of focus, where the different forces are in balance. Here Degas seeks to poise the dancer or the horse, for here absolute equilibrium conquers motion and other disruptive forces. This critical point had to be determined with precision, and once it was determined, the artist pounced on it, pinning it down almost as if he had used a drawing compass.

Transfixed by his implacable attention, Degas' models are poised frozen in motion—but are made vibrant with color. Despite his emphasis on line, brilliant hues invaded his pictures, replacing the dark tones of his earlier work. As he grew older his color often became more feverish than that of his Impressionist colleagues; but unlike theirs, it does not abolish the boundaries of form and engage in free play. It remains local, trapped within the limits of the dancer's tutu or the jockey's silks.

Compasses make deadly weapons—the artist himself had compared the making of a painting to "the perpetration of a crime." For Degas, walled up in his solitude, art was a form of compensation, of aggression, of vengeance. "Art is vice," he said; "one doesn't wed it legitimately, one rapes it." He grants ugly women a degree of attention they had rarely received from painters; and he often catches them in particularly ungainly postures: yawning, scratching, scrubbing in tubs or squatting on bidets. These are activities seldom practiced in public. Their revelation is an invasion of privacy. And indeed, as Degas told the English writer George Moore, he wanted to show "the human beast" (the very phrase Zola used as a title for one of his novels) "as if you were looking through a keyhole." Degas does not merely look at women; he seems to stare at them with a fanatic intensity that borders on voyeurism (significantly, he never formed a lasting intimate relationship with a woman).

By the early 1880s Degas had started losing his eyesight, and to compensate for the growing darkness he increasingly worked with pastels and heightened the brilliance of his colors. It could be said that tragedy freed his colors. In his late works, smoldering fires devoured all forms. And finally, he could not work at all. Yet he was to live for many more painful years. Barricaded behind his misanthropy, nearly blind but loath to accept it, he wandered aimlessly around Paris, in constant danger of being run over, an old Homer without his lyre. Death delivered him at last, on September 27, 1917.

Both as a man and as an artist, Manet was the complete antithesis of Degas. They sprang from the same heritage, they shared a passion for the city, and they were fitful friends for many years, but there the similarities stopped. "Nothing could be less spontaneous than my art," Degas had said. "An artist has to be a spontaneist," said Manet. No rules, no calculations, no precautions for Manet; every time he started a painting was the first time. Just as he splashed about in Paris life with as much joy at 50 as at 20, so the paintings of the '70s have the immediacy of the unprecedented. Manet is one of the few masters who escape being trapped in a defined, consistent style. Each painting was a matter of sink or swim—and more than once, he sank; Degas was never more firmly on solid ground than when he seemed to lean way out.

These oppositions show up most glaringly in those years when Degas' and Manet's works are so close in subject matter. Time and again, the two artists concern themselves with the same themes: the horse races *(pages 74-75 and 152-153)*, popular singers performing at *café-concerts (pages 146 and 157)*, men and women drinking in *brasseries (pages 148-149 and 156)*. In some instances they actually pictured the same models, as happened with the bohemian artist Marcellin Desboutin and the actress Ellen Andrée.

While Manet mostly depicted scenes such as those of pleasure and leisure, he was also deeply interested in the serious, industrial aspects of contemporary life. In 1873 he had tackled the theme of the railroad, albeit indirectly: the machine's presence in *The Railway* manifests itself only through the wisps of smoke rising behind the figure of the little girl and her companion. He intended also to treat the subject more directly. He traveled from Versailles to Paris on a locomotive, watching the engineer and the fireman. "Theirs is a dog's life," he reported to an acquaintance during a bout of illness. "These men are modern heroes. When I am better, I will paint them."

He included this subject among those listed in his plan for decorating Paris' new City Hall. He applied for the commission in a letter to the Prefect of the Seine; he proposed to adorn the walls of the council chamber with compositions illustrating the Zolaesque theme of "The Belly of Paris." The Prefect did not even bother to reply. In fact, the only decoration for a public building that Manet ever had a part in was *The Civil Marriage*, executed by an academic painter, Henri Gervex, for the town hall of Ménilmontant. Manet posed for one of the figures.

No artist was ever less accounted for by labels than Manet—all the more when the label was an ambiguous term coined in connection with literature and later extended to painting. Thus one should take with a grain of salt the affirmation, often heard, that the difference between the Manet of the '60s and the Manet of the '70s was a shift (punctuated by the brief Impressionist holiday at Argenteuil) from Realism to Naturalism. But there is some truth in the statement. The Naturalist novel analyzed industry, the masses and the garish pleasures of the city, in which it saw the degradation inflicted upon the poor by the pitiless machine of society. Manet's locomotives, his prostitutes and his urban crowds are also familiar ingredients of Zola's novels, and his pictures of the *café-concert* life are reminiscent of the descriptions of the theatrical world found in the Naturalist writings of Zola's most talented disciple, J. K. Huysmans. But of Zola's pseudoscientific doctrine, of his sociobiological "experiments" and demonstrations, not a trace is to be seen in Manet's paintings.

The difference between Realism and Naturalism—subtle at best— was expressed not so much in the difference of subject matter as in its treatment. Both schools are concerned with facts, but Realism selects its facts and loads them with moral meanings—Courbet, for example, was interested in their social implications; Naturalism presents more facts, simply as they met the artist's eye. The Realist will describe two men drinking, the Naturalist will point out that the one is drinking wine while the other is drinking beer—and he will stress the dissimilarity between the two states of inebriety. In this respect, Manet by the 1870s has definitely evolved from Realism to Naturalism.

The difference becomes apparent when we compare *The Absinthe Drinker (page 29)* with any of the treatments of the drinking theme in the 1870s—say *The Plum (page 148)*, or *At the Café (page 149)*. In the former, facts are reduced to the minimum; reality—the dress, the props —is pared down, stylized to the point where the drinker might be as much at home in the time of Murillo as in that of Courbet. Nor is the background any help in placing him: it is a blank wall. In the later canvases, however, we have no trouble in placing the scene in time and space. These men and women could not have lived except around 1880; these cafés flourished at no other epoch.

In the later pictures Manet has tried, in short, to convey far more information than in the earlier ones. We not only learn that the subjects drink, but what they drink: on the counter of *A Bar at the Folies-Bergère* are bottles of a beer still obtainable—as we see from the labels—in pubs today. On the walls of the houses shown in *Rue Mosnier Decked with Flags (page 146)* are posters, reminding us of the fact that these were the years when colorful advertising invaded the streets of Paris. Manet also seeks now to provide us with psychological information about his models: whereas in *The Balcony (page 76)* or *The Luncheon (page 77)* the figures are isolated, the pair in *Chez le Père Lathuille (page 147)* are unequivocally the protagonists of flirtation between young, fatuous beau and not quite so young and no longer so beauteous lady. Manet thus strews his Naturalistic pictures with clear, unambiguous clues. So great is his eagerness to identify his models that in *The Masked Ball at the Opera*, where all the men are dressed alike, he combats this anonymity by tilting each top hat at an angle inimitably personal to its owner.

Why this need to identify precisely the content of his pictures? Because he realized more and more clearly that two-dimensional paint contained a fatal threat to the identity of the people and objects represented. The bold elision of such masterpieces of the 1860s as *The Fifer (page 56)*, in which content is reduced to a simplified figure against a simplified background, had testified to Manet's knowledge that two-dimensional composition would only "take" a modest amount of information.

Under the influence of the Impressionists, however, Manet had adopted another way of painting: he pelted the canvas with a hailstorm of short, nervous dapples of pigment. This technique risked even more complete disintegration of the discrete, identifiable image. Such dissolution of form is what lends particular poignancy to a portrait Claude Monet painted of his wife Camille on her deathbed. Try as he would, he could no more prevent her image from dissolving into a whirl of brushstrokes than he could save her from the disintegration of death. Normally Monet welcomed the chromatic break-up, in which he saw the pictorial transcription of optical fact. But for Manet, who was less concerned with the laws of optics, it also meant just what it is: visible strokes of the brush on a surface. And to counterweigh the increased threat to identity contained in this looser manner of painting, he increased the load of information to be conveyed by other elements of the picture.

There was downright heroism in the undertaking. No one knew better than Manet that reality, when observed and depicted from the outside, can become merely prosaic. To escape this fate, reality must be painted *in* the present, not just looked at but lived, set ablaze in a flash of recognition. Furthermore no one knew better that a match catches fire more easily than a tree trunk. It was possible to reconcile pure paint with a single face or figure or with an isolated stalk of asparagus; could it be done with the quantity of material—colors, forms, objects and the distances between them—that Manet now imposed on his canvases? In his Realistic pictures, he had, so to speak, turned telegrams into songs; in his Naturalistic ones, it was a matter of turning newspaper prose into melody. At times he failed; at others, he succeeded in fusing the present of history and the present of paint into incandescent unity.

I t was in these years, the mid-'70s, that Manet painted the picture that may be considered a symbol of his artistic drama: *Before the Mirror (pages 9-11)*. In the looking glass, we see paint, not the woman's image. The coherent unity that would have enabled us to recognize her has been broken up into a multiplicity of brushstrokes. These brushstrokes do not "mean" anything except their own existence as paint. The loosening up of the pictorial fabric into swarming dots and dashes dissolved the oneness of the represented form into a plurality—Impressionism's technique of dappling—that no longer formed the image of a subject but that imposed an awareness of the literal act of painting. The roses in his still life *Roses and Lilacs* irresistibly conjure up the coherence of fresh flowers; but the disintegrated flecks on the table, which are intended to signify wilted, fallen petals, look, first and foremost, like dabs of paint.

This was an awkward predicament for an artist who wished paint to

The collector who bought Manet's lovely, small still life of a bunch of asparagus *(above)* was so delighted with his purchase that he paid the artist 200 francs more than the agreed price. Manet, in turn, was so flattered by this appreciation that he dashed off another painting of a single spear *(below)* and sent it to the buyer with his compliments and the whimsical explanation, "There was one missing from your bunch."

be, but also to mean. What subject could the plurality of paint possibly stand for? It was here that Manet's profound sense of the city stood him in good stead. He had grasped intuitively that the dominant characteristic of the modern metropolis is the crowd. *Concert in the Tuileries* had superbly exploited this theme. Now, more than 15 years later, he saw that it provided him with a way to reorganize painterly disintegration into a meaningful pattern: wasn't the crowd a plurality that threatened to drown the individual exactly as the plurality of paint— those myriad brushstrokes—threatened to dissolve the coherence of the identifiable image?

When taken at face value—that is, as it stands on the picture's surface—any area of color ranks with any other; on the picture plane, an orange is as important as a face (more so perhaps). Two-dimensionality destroys the normal hierarchies of emphasis: just so, individuals are absorbed in the collective entity of the human mass. Here, then, was the subject that allowed Manet's paintings to go on doing what pictures had done since the Renaissance: to represent.

Many of Manet's pictures executed after 1875 derive their tension from the dramatic confrontation of fragile individuality with boundless multitude, or—to put it in artistic terms—of identifiable image with irrepressible paint. Never was paint more freely and boldly dispensed than in the fiery waves of the vast ocean surrounding Rochefort and his companions in their small boat in Manet's *The Escape of Rochefort*. Like *The Execution of the Emperor Maximilian*, it is a political picture, a tribute by the liberal Manet to the radical politician and journalist Henri de Rochefort, who was sentenced to life imprisonment and deported to New Caledonia after the government crushed the Commune in 1871. Rochefort escaped in a small boat, made his way to the United States and returned to Paris after a general amnesty was granted by the Third Republic in 1880. (The following year Manet painted a portrait of his hero that Rochefort—born a marquis, and no lover of modern art—refused.) Like *Maximilian*, the *Escape* unconsciously shifts ground: just as the underlying theme of *Maximilian* is the assassination of narrative, so the real theme of *The Escape of Rochefort* is the hopelessly uneven exposure of the one to the many.

This confrontation of the one and the many injects undertones of pathos into a number of apparently carefree pictures by Manet. In *The Promenade*, a woman stands out isolated, alone against the multiplicity of the foliage in the background. It was the plural character of the foliage, as of the sea, that mattered to Manet. Often, as in *Skating* and in *The Masked Ball at the Opera*, the individual in Manet's pictures is a woman, again alone, in a crowd chiefly composed of men.

Baudelaire had spoken of Manet's "decided taste for reality, modern reality." It was more than a taste. Manet had a fundamental insight into the nature of two urgent modern preoccupations: the loss of individuality in the flood of ever-growing urban crowds, and, in art, the progressive elimination of image and subject matter. In the best of his late works Manet achieved a fusion of these two concerns with a profoundness that to this day has not been surpassed.

Manet, Degas and the City

In the 1870s, Manet again turned with delight to painting the scenes and subjects he liked best: Paris, and Parisians everywhere they appeared—on the streets, at cafés, in gardens, boudoirs and salons. By choosing the life of his city, Manet was also choosing a course that led him away from Monet, Renoir, Sisley, Pissarro and the other nonconformist painters who, as Impressionists, concentrated largely on capturing the fleeting effects of light and color in sun-dappled landscapes.

Of the old companions, only Degas was as interested as Manet in urban subjects. That these particular men should stand apart was almost inevitable. For Manet and Degas were both cool, worldly sons of cultivated Paris families and in their work, as well as their temperaments, they retained a certain detachment of their class. Of course, they borrowed from the Impressionists, at times adopting the technique of quick brushstrokes of pure color. But they also found a new perception of their surroundings in photography and Japanese art and refused to confine themselves to any rigid doctrine. Degas even worked long and hard on sculpture. Above all, Manet and Degas enjoyed their sophisticated, booming Paris especially its racetracks, ballet theatres and concert halls. Coming back to the city after an absence of some months, Degas explained both himself and his friend: "One loves and endows with art only what one is accustomed to . . . Three cheers for fine French laundering."

With *Nana*, Manet again became a victim of Paris gossip. The public cried scandal at seeing the half-clad, saucy woman obviously preparing for an evening's diversion with the waiting gentleman. In 1876, Nana appeared as a minor character in one of Zola's serialized stories; in 1877, Manet painted this "portrait"; in 1879, Zola published a full-length novel. Manet seems to have been inspired by his writer friend's creation.

Nana, 1877

Rue Mosnier Decked with Flags, 1878

The Café-Concert, 1879

Chez le Père Lathuille, 1879

In his Paris scenes, Manet used a variety of techniques to illustrate the life around him. By the arresting omission of happy throngs and the inclusion of a solitary cripple he turned a golden street on a national holiday into a strangely quiet and disturbing place *(left, above)*. With a flurry of Impressionist brushstrokes, and not one clear feature, he described the tough vitality of a singer entertaining diners at a fashionable garden café *(left)*. By restraint, both in color and emotional tone, he made a tender moment of what could have been a tawdry scene between an intense young dandy and an older woman *(above)*. In the two paintings on the following pages, Manet brushed delicate colors into his softly modeled portraits of women at café bars, seeing beyond such devastating details as the dangling cigarettes into their wistful eyes—perhaps to suggest their empty lives.

147

The Plum, 1877

At the Café, 1878

149

Degas

Degas, *Self-portrait*, c. 1854-1855

Edgar-Hilaire-Germain Degas was born July 19, 1834, two years after Manet —and 20 years before he painted the self-portrait at the left. He was always a private individual, as his cool young eyes indicate, perhaps because his Creole mother, who came from a prominent family of cotton brokers in New Orleans, died when he was only 14. Degas' two brothers joined the family cotton business, and he kept in touch with his American relatives; during a visit to America, he painted his uncle (the foreground figure wearing a stovepipe hat) and his brothers (one reading a newspaper, the other leaning on the window), in the scene below. Degas' father, a distinguished banker who became withdrawn after his wife's early death, is at the right in his son's portrait of the guitarist, Pagans, playing in the family's Paris home.

Degas, *The Cotton Exchange at New Orleans*, 1873

150

Degas, *The Guitarist Pagans and Monsieur Degas*, c. 1869

Degas, *Race Horses, at Longchamp*, 1873-1875

Throughout his career, Degas had a passion for painting living forms in motion. He never considered horses as creatures to love (a confirmed nonathlete, Degas did not even ride); they attracted him as living machinery: arrangements of fleshed joints that moved in marvelous patterns. He first began painting race horses after visiting his father's wealthy friends, the Valpinçons, at their château in Normandy. The Valpinçons' stables were among the most notable in a region famous as horse-breeding, race-meeting country, and the 27-year-old Degas, now seeing the animals at close range, was instantly fascinated by their elegant mobility. Thereafter he often wandered with his sketchbook wherever horses were to be found—in stables, at exercise and, especially, at the racetrack—until he knew every rippling muscle,

every bone, all the quick and unexpected attitudes of "this wonderful piece of mechanism." From many hundreds of sketches—only some 250 remain—came such paintings as the superb rear views of horses in action, at left, and the vivid studies of the different positions a horse will assume, below.

In Degas' eyes, women, too, were "wonderful pieces of mechanism" that crouched, turned, gaped, stretched and lifted with grace—especially when, lost in work or in privacy, they moved in habitual, almost automatic, routines. The next two pages show how Degas painted women deprived of affectations: a customer examining a hat at her milliner's, laundresses working at an ironing table, a nude contorted as she bends for a sponge in her low English-style bath tub.

Degas, *At the Races Before the Start*, 1878-1880

Degas, *The Millinery Shop*, 1885

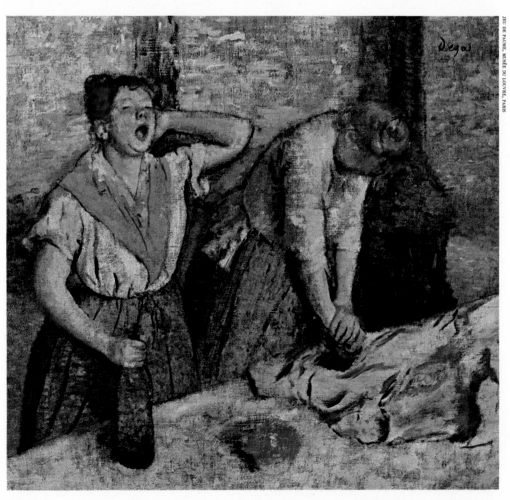

Degas, *Women Ironing*, c. 1884

Degas, *Woman in the Tub*, c. 1886

Degas, *Absinthe*, c. 1877

Degas, *Café-Concert at the Ambassadeurs*, c.1876-1877

Like Manet, Degas was fascinated by the men and women who frequented the cafés of Paris, and he often used friends to model for his café scenes—sometimes mutual friends. At left, the impoverished engraver Marcellin Desboutin poses with the actress Ellen Andrée, who had agreed to sit for Manet's *Chez le Père Lathuille (page 147)* but reneged when she got a part in a play. The scene is the Café de la Nouvelle Athènes, which may also have served Manet as a setting for *The Plum (page 148).*

In both the pictures shown here Degas chose cameralike points of view, placing his main figures off-center and deftly suggesting spaces much larger than he shows. At left, the slanting lines of the table edges not only lead the eye right to his subjects, but beyond, to other, unseen, drinkers. Above, the low perspective places the viewer directly in the middle of the audience, and the singer, almost obscured by the bass-fiddle neck, gestures to other, unseen, listeners. Thus, with a brush as sharp as a scalpel, Degas has cut slices of reality out of life and fixed them forever in the mind.

COLLECTION OF MR. AND MRS. NORTON SIMON

Degas, *Ballet Rehearsal*, 1875

The same disciplined beauty of movement that attracted Degas to horses also drew him to his most famous subjects, girls of the ballet. Audiences see ballet dancers as ethereal beings of another world, delicate and lighter than air. Degas saw them as skinny creatures of muscle and bone whose apparent grace and lightness are the end product of incredibly hard work. To translate this revelation into pictures, Degas scrupulously observed dancers backstage, at classes and rehearsals, as well as during performances. In close observation of ballet people —the old dancers who had become teachers, the poor young girls, called "rats," in the back lines of the chorus —he found the quality of movement he had been searching for since the early days of painting horses. So intently did Degas study his subjects that he could recall the most subtle detail of what he had seen in the theater from only a few sketches and notes. In the painting above, the girl in the left foreground bends with a true ballet dancer's awkward posture as she massages an aching ankle —and the ballet master, though old, stands as straight as when he was a leading dancer. Degas' accurate eye also saw the personalities of his "rats," although he was never really interested in portraying the drama of their lives. At right, on a stage aswirl with elegant disciplined legs and tulle-swathed torsos, the sly face of a girl who might be a concierge's daughter peers into the glow of footlights.

Degas, *Ballet Seen From a Box*, 1885

Degas, *Dancers at the Bar*, c. 1888

Degas, *Melina Darde Seated*, 1878

Degas' ballet pastels are so spontaneous that they seem to have been made on the spot. Actually he worked in his studio, posing off-duty dancers from his precise memory, aided only by quick but specific sketches like the one above. Here, as his verbal notes indicate, he has drawn the 15-year-old ballerina of the Gaiety Theatre, Melina Darde, as she exercises her ankles in the "point" position. At the upper right he observed that "the top of her head is covered with a spray of fine hairs except in back." In his finished studies, Degas often used pastel colors because, being both dry and opaque, they enabled him to work swiftly, to retouch and experiment with bright harmonies. He also sometimes reworked the dusty, soft pastel finish by blowing steam over the surface, moistening the colors, and then using a stiff brush to create even more delicate tones.

Degas, *Ballet Dancer, Dressed*, 1880-1881

Degas turned to sculpture primarily as an exercise in the creation of form, but he worked with the originality that marked his genius. Here is his unusual figure of a dancer, a 39-inch-high statuette that caused an uproar at the Impressionists' exhibition in 1881. Critics objected not only to the girl's impudent, inelegant pose, but to her sculptured flesh, which Degas had painted, and her clothes, which were real—a tulle *tutu*, a cloth bodice, soft shoes and silk ribbon. Achieving an extraordinary realism, Degas, in the critics' eyes, had created "an ideal of ugliness." He never again exhibited sculpture.

Degas, *Woman Washing Her Left Leg*, c. 1896-1911

Degas fingerprints can still be seen in the bronzes that were cast from his wax and clay originals after his death. Impatient with technique—he received but largely ignored the advice of sculptors—Degas cared less about the permanence of the pieces that he modeled than their success as studies of three-dimensional reality. When he died, in September 1917, some 150 small sculptures were found in his studio. Many were broken or crumbling. Only 30 were as complete as the Spanish dancer and bathing woman shown here.

Degas, *Spanish Dance*, c. 1882-1895

With the exception of the clothed ballerina, all Degas' sculptures are small—usually under 20 inches. His horses, therefore, are the more remarkable, for while being small they nevertheless give the impression of full size and great power. The horse pawing the earth below is less than eight inches high; the rearing beast at right is just over a foot tall: riderless and free, they express all that Degas loved in them. Indeed, horses were the first subjects that attracted Degas in sculpture, as they had in painting. So well had he come to know them through his racetrack sketches that he could probably model a horse from memory. This was fortunate, for Degas' eyes began to fail him when he was about 40, and they got progressively worse. Sculpture, first of horses, then of dancers and bathers, must have given him welcome relief from the strains of painting.

Degas, *Horse with Head Lowered*, c. 1865-1881

Degas, *Rearing Horse*, c. 1865-1881

Letters to Isabelle

While convalescing in the country at Bellevue during the summers of 1879 and 1880, Manet wrote a number of affectionate letters to young Isabelle Lemonnier, 28 years his junior, and illustrated them with charming sketches. On the opposite page are *(from top)* some Bastille Day flags, a drowsy cat and a "philippine" nut with two kernels, a symbol of love or friendship. Below is a sketch of Isabelle herself and a deft drawing of a mirabelle plum, accompanied by Manet's bit of verse:

> *To Isabelle,*
> *That mirabelle,*
> *to the loveliest,*
> *That's Isabelle.*

And indeed, he was sometimes very close to despair. For the doctors had finally had to disclose to Manet that he suffered not from rheumatism but from locomotor ataxia, a ruinous disorder of the nervous system that sometimes accompanies the later stages of syphilis. Its painful effects are relentlessly progressive; Manet's trouble with his foot was just the beginning of a dreadful siege of incurable sickness.

To forget his miseries he tried to work; but unable to summon the necessary strength and concentration, he would give up in disgust. He turned increasingly to still lifes, partly out of regard for the form—he had once said that "still life is the touchstone of painting"—but also because he now had to limit himself to small canvases as a consequence of ill health. His subject matter too reflects his precarious condition: fruit, vegetables and, above all, flowers—things of the most perishable kind. Renoir's blossoming girls and flowers seem blessed with eternal youth; Manet's lilacs and roses are the more brilliant for being manifestly destined to wilt. The price of their incredible freshness is fragility—such fragility as Manet now knew to be his lot. His weakness even influenced his choice of a medium; unable to sustain beyond brief sessions the tension of working with his accustomed passionate involvement, he tended more and more to restrict himself to watercolor, a medium that not only permitted but actually called for brevity.

Many of these watercolors were done as illustrations for short letters sent by the artist to his friends. "I send you two plums from my garden and my friendly greetings," he wrote the baritone Faure. For the most part lighthearted and frivolous, these notes, often addressed to women, were exquisite substitutes for the gallant compliments he usually delivered so gracefully in person.

Among them, the letters to Isabelle Lemonnier have a special place. She was the young sister of Madame Charpentier, whose husband, Georges, was a publisher and art collector. Isabelle, from an upper-middle-class family in the Manets' circle, was only 19 in 1879 when he first painted her, but she obviously very much attracted the artist. He had painted her several times. Now, in his green prison in Bellevue, Manet's thoughts turned to Isabelle again and again, and clearly his interest was more than simply artistic. "I would kiss you, had I the courage," he wrote on one occasion.

Behind the façade of a playful, avuncular flirtation, one can sense the poignant nostalgia that a man shaken and aged by illness feels for the freshness of youth. Manet sent her sketches *(page 168)*—almost Oriental in their swift, elliptic assurance—of flowers, people, fruit. A cat accompanied the following note: "This is a little hello in passing. I would like to receive one every morning, when the mail arrives. But I am afraid that you like your friends less than I do. . . ." Manet redoubled his pleas, at times almost plaintively: "You certainly don't spoil me. Either you are very busy, or you are very nasty." But Isabelle was neither nasty nor busy; she was indifferent, deaf with the deafness of her youth to the distress of her famous, middle-aged admirer. As a result, Manet was forced to make up what she would not tell him. Because he knew that she was vacationing with her parents at the seaside, he sketched her standing ready to dive, or plunging into the surf. After reading newspaper reports about the fireworks and other festivities with which Isabelle's family celebrated the 14th of July—1880 was the year in which Bastille Day became a national holiday—he depicted, with a few delicate brushstrokes, Chinese lanterns and tricolored flags. But the images had no more effect than the words. Isabelle, and through her, life itself, turned away from him.

Back in Paris that autumn, Manet hurled himself anew into the hectic life of the *boulevardier*, as if to convince himself and others that he was well again, although the improvement in his condition—if it really *did* improve—was no more than a temporary respite. His motto was: pleasure as usual. He ordered his mother and his wife to resume their practice of regular musical parties and receptions. He himself was "at home" in his studio at the usual hours. To celebrate his renewal of energy, Manet painted two canvases, the large-scale portrait of the explorer Pertuiset and *The Escape of Rochefort* (he actually executed two pictures on this theme). But his strength went no further, and again his fury to paint confined itself to small-sized works.

Manet sent *Pertuiset* and a portrait of Rochefort to the Salon of 1881. The State had just turned over the control of the Salon to an autonomous society of artists, a change that did not imply a true liberalization, for the jury still contained some die-hard reactionaries. Indeed, Manet's entries would have been rejected on both artistic and political grounds (a portrait of the radical Communard Rochefort struck many jurors as a downright provocation), had it not been for the sudden, entirely unexpected support of an arch conservative member of the jury, Alexandre Cabanel. His traditional *Birth of Venus* 18 years before had won the applause of the same Salon that had rejected *Luncheon on the Grass*, but now he was in Manet's camp. Cabanel's outburst in praise of Manet—"There are not four of us here capable of doing so well," he exclaimed—so influenced his colleagues on the jury that Manet was awarded a prized second-class medal. At last the prize that had been Manet's dream for 20 years was his. Henceforth his pictures would bear the label "H.C.," for *hors concours*, or "out of competition," and he could exhibit at the Salon without having to secure the approval of the jury.

Yet he did not savor the satisfaction as fully as he might have a few years earlier. He suffered, and he was exhausted. In the summer of 1881 he rented a villa with a small garden, near the park of Versailles. He hoped, once he felt better, to paint its classical perspectives and he took exploratory walks in it. But he did not feel better, and soon he was forced to give up these strolls and to restrict himself, both corporally and pictorially, to the limits of his garden. "Having come here with the intention of doing studies in the park designed by Lenôtre," he wrote a friend, "I have been forced simply to paint my garden, the most hideous of gardens." When asked by Mallarmé to illustrate his translation of some poems by Edgar Allan Poe, Manet wrote disconsolately: "You know how much I like to embark with you on any kind of work; but these days it is beyond my strength."

From time to time the creative spirit flared up in him; he would then dash off a view of his garden. But these landscapes of his late years are different from the bright, cheerful views of his Impressionistic phase at Argenteuil. There is something ominous about their luxuriance. The foliage looks green but feels almost black; it is thick to the point of impenetrability, a vegetal wall no less restrictive than the stone wall that marked the boundaries of the artist's shrinking universe. Summer had turned its back on Manet, and in retrospect it is easy to sense in his work an echo of the despair of these unhappy days. *The Promenade*, painted a year earlier at Bellevue, takes on tragic overtones not only because the lone figure of the woman is pitted against the multitude of leaves, like Rochefort isolated amidst waves, but also because she stands against the wall of foliage—and walls, in Manet's work, are places for executions.

That summer in Versailles even imaginary convalescence was slow to come, yet when Manet returned to Paris in October, he sought once again to present in public his customary visage of carefree exuberance. But the strain told, and at home he grew increasingly moody, nervous and taciturn. Still, he showed up at the familiar haunts: cafés like Tortoni's and the Bade, and the Folies-Bergère. It was at the Folies that he conceived a last monumental project—a large painting of its huge mirrored bar. This picture was to occupy him for several months and would consume a heavy share of his flagging artistic energy.

At least one pleasure—albeit a bittersweet one—came to Manet that winter while he was working with difficulty on the picture. Gambetta, the new Prime Minister, had just made Antonin Proust his Minister of Fine Arts. Proust suggested that Manet receive the Legion of Honor, and Gambetta, who was acquainted with Manet, readily agreed. When the Premier presented the list of *chevaliers*-to-be to the President of the Republic, Jules Grévy, for approval, that dignitary burst out: "Manet! Not that! Never!" It took Gambetta's stern insistence to get him to underwrite the nomination; on December 30, Manet was notified of the honor. In other days, he would have been overjoyed. Now, it was as with his second-class medal at the Salon: he could no longer enjoy his triumph fully. When a critic conveyed to him the congratulations of Count de Nieuwerkerke, the erstwhile Superintendent of Fine Arts to Napoleon III, Manet replied: "When you write to him, tell him that I am touched by his kind thought but that he could have decorated me. He could have made my fortune; and now, it is too late to repair twenty years' lack of success."

Hampered by his inability to make a sustained effort, Manet made slow progress on *A Bar at the Folies-Bergère (pages 177-183)*. More and more often, he would interrupt his work and throw himself, pale and trembling, on a couch near his easel in a state of exhaustion. Still, he finished the picture in time for the Salon in May. For the first—and, as it turned out, the only—time, he did not have to subject himself to the whim of the jury. Nevertheless the critics, unimpressed by the "H.C." accompanying it, were reserved about the *Bar*, which one of them called "an indecipherable puzzle." Even Degas found it "subtle and tedious."

Yet all the concerns of a lifetime converge on this large canvas to make it a climactic masterpiece.

At first glance, *Bar* appears simple enough. A barmaid, standing exactly in the center of the picture, looks at us across a marble counter cluttered with bottles of whisky, ale, champagne and liqueurs, a glass holding two roses and a fruit bowl filled with oranges. The girl is young and attractive; the place, the hour, the occasion speak of frivolity, of merrymaking. Yet there is something strangely solemn about *Bar*, as if the celebration depicted were that of a sacrifice. The waitress seems to rise like an expiatory victim, not over bottles of beer and champagne, but above candles on an altar. Perhaps it is because she seems fragile, vulnerable, despite her grandness.

The fragility is on her face, in which professional attentiveness barely hides exhaustion. It is also in the many symbols of ephemerality that surround her, the perishable fruit and flowers, the dissipating wisps of smoke, the lights that will soon be turned off. It is in the minute observation of how things and people looked at one precise, passing moment in history and at no other. But above all, the sense of fragility stems from the picture's composition. What lends the girl her monumental presence is also what endangers her: she is in the singular, so to speak, while everything else—the bottles, the spectators, the lights— is in the plural. Plurality threatens to devour her. Despite her size and central position, we cannot easily focus on her, for she is already on her way to being dispersed—she appears a second time, quite asymmetrically, in the mirror behind her.

Perhaps you had not noticed the mirror: that is because it occupies the entire background of the picture. As a result, the background is really the foreground, i.e., the side where *we* are. Instead of luring our eyes into the imaginary recesses on the picture's other side, Manet encourages us to view the scene as if it were taking place on our side, and to participate directly in it. The apparent elimination of background is only one step that Manet took to restrict space in this picture. Intensifying effects he had used in earlier paintings, he squeezed the waitress between the mirror and the counter, that is to say, between the "wall" and the surface of the picture. Station is emphasized at the expense of action. In fact, it takes a good deal of looking to discover what action there is; that, for instance, a performance is going on at the moment, revealed by the swinging legs of a trapeze artist near the upper left corner of the canvas. We are worlds away from the fascination with motion that governs Degas in his pictures of similar events. And psychological expression is played down no less than physical gesticulation: like most of the figures portrayed by Manet, the waitress is utterly impassive.

What we see in the mirror is less the acrobat's act than the audience that is looking at it. Once again Manet has expressed multiplicity of the crowd with the multiplicity of paint. And from the mirror quick dabs of darkish pigment spill out onto the marble counter, lapping at the bottles, the glasses, the silhouette of the customer at the right, the girl's dress, and we are made to feel that its growing tide will soon swallow up the girl's face as it did that of the dying Camille in Monet's picture.

Yet Manet, by disposition a conservative, is the first to be terrified by the revolution he has wrought. He does his utmost to combat the turmoil he has stirred up. His desire to rescue identity from the tidal wave of paint has caused him to knit the fabric of the barmaid's face tightly, whereas everywhere else the brush darts about freely and loosely. On the brink of disintegration, the picture recollects itself around her. Concentration on one person staves off dispersion—exactly as the sight of a single face standing out in the flow of passersby relieves us for a time of the anxiety of dilution in the modern crowd. The first man to have grasped this typically modern situation was Manet's friend Baudelaire. In his poem *The Passerby*, he described just such a sidewalk epiphany. "A lightning stroke. . .then night—Fugitive beauty," he wrote. A fugitive beauty torn from night by a dazzling flash of recognition—such is the heroine of *A Bar at the Folies-Bergère*. Here, quite miraculously, Manet has set ablaze a chunk of reality so large as to seem almost incombustible. It has the grandeur of the transcendent and the fragility of the transient. The moment turns into monument. *A Bar at the Folies-Bergère* is the sum, the summary and the summit of Manet's lifelong endeavor.

Summer came to Paris again, and the Manets rented a villa at Rueil, near the city. Small as its garden was, Manet could not hobble around it save at the cost of excruciating pain. Most of the time, he remained confined to his armchair, reading cloak-and-dagger novels, too listless even to reply to the letters of his friends. "It takes all the friendship I feel toward you to make me write," he tells Méry. In another note to her, he laments: "I need to work to feel well." But his condition made it almost impossible; a couple of views of his house and garden, a handful of still lifes make up the entire summer's production. Just before leaving Rueil to return to Paris, he drew up his will. His temper grew steadily more sour. "One should not bring children into the world when one makes them like this!" he bitterly reproached his mother.

And still, hope clutched at the slightest symptom of remission. It was during such a truce that he conceived the idea for a portrait of a woman in riding habit. If the *Bar* had been his artistic testament, this work was an ultimate codicil. That fall or winter, he went for an outing in the Bois de Boulogne—though it is doubtful that he could any longer stroll for very long in any comfort—and there he saw a woman riding. She wore a black riding coat and a black top hat. Back in his studio, Manet called for a model, whom he dressed in the same attire. The result is the portrait of a woman, Manet's favorite symbol for individuality; but the hat and coat are the uniform of men, his symbol for the crowd. *Young Woman in Riding Costume*, Manet's final vision, offered a swift, lyrical solution to the conflict between unity and plurality so fully and dramatically stated in *A Bar at the Folies-Bergère*.

As was his custom when dealing with an important motif, Manet executed several versions of the horsewoman. One day, while working on the last one in the presence of a friend, he tottered, moaned and collapsed on the floor. When at last he was able to stand up, he seized his palette knife and slashed the canvas. Henceforth, he was to paint only fruit and flowers. Flowers! "I would like to paint them all," he sighed. It was an ancient passion with him, now magnified by the fact that he could indulge in no other. Aware of this, his friends showered him with bouquets and some of these found their way onto canvas—a branch of lilac, roses in a glass, carnations, peonies.

Never does the flame of life seem to burn more brightly than when it is on the verge of extinction, and the freshness and radiance of these last works, both watercolors and oils, are truly extraordinary. The corollas, the stems of the flowers, are held together by the frailest of threads; the petals explode from an infinitesimal focus of energy. Irresistibly, the eye is carried to that vital center—only to discover that it is a blank, a void. As a rose is aglow with the imminence of its decay, so the images of Manet's roses sparkle and quiver with the manifest signs of their dissolution into pure paint.

The great revolution that occurs in Manet's work—paint's rebellion against its age-old role as a mirror—is here reduced to its starkest, simplest expression. Is it the asparagus we perceive first, or the bold strokes of the brush? The identifiable image hesitates before tumbling into the silent ocean of paint. Manet's late pictures of fruit and flowers capture all the brilliance and poignancy of this supreme moment of suspension preceding the fall.

On February 28, 1883, Manet painted white lilacs in a glass; on March 1, he painted a bouquet of roses. They were his last finished pictures. Three weeks later, Méry's maid, Elisa, arrived, as she did almost every day, with flowers sent by her mistress. Manet quickly began a pastel portrait of her; that night he left his studio for his home, and he was not to rise again from his bed.

His left foot began to turn gray: gangrene had set in. The "old fighter," as Renoir had called him, was waging his last battle with the same courage he had shown in his attacks against academic art. In the desperate hope of working despite his dwindling strength, he asked a specialist in miniature painting to give him lessons. But it was too late even for that. The gangrene was gaining fast. On the urgent advice of his physicians, Manet agreed to have his left leg amputated, and the operation took place at 10 o'clock in the morning on April 19 in the Manets' drawing room. Such was the general emotion and confusion that the leg, severed just below the knee, was thrown into the fireplace, where it was found some time later.

At first, the health bulletin tacked daily to the concierge's door—there was great curiosity about the fate of a well-known Parisian figure like Manet—indicated improvement. Monet was able to visit his old comrade; when he put his cap on Manet's bed, the latter indicated his missing left leg and cried in anguish, "Careful! You'll hurt my foot!"

Soon, however, fever set in, followed by delirium. On Sunday the 29th, the final agony began, accompanied by terrible suffering. "An appalling death!. . .Death in one of its most horrible aspects," lamented Berthe Morisot. Édouard Manet died, at the age of 52, on Monday, April 30, 1883—the day before the opening of the Salon.

A Final Triumph

In 1881, when the Folies-Bergère night club in Paris was only 12 years old and was just beginning to win world fame for its spectacular stage shows and grand tableaux, Manet used it as the setting for the greatest of his late paintings, *Bar at the Folies-Bergère*. The work proceeded under the most painful circumstances, for the artist had entered the final, energy-sapping phase of locomotor ataxia, the disease that would end his life in two years at 52. Compounding the difficulties, his illness confined him for at least part of each year to serenely quiet retreats outside Paris, where he was isolated from the festive flush of city life that had sustained him for so long. Perhaps it was in homage to the gay world beyond his ebbing energies that he selected the bright, crowded variety hall as the scene for this picture.

Manet chose for the focus of his painting not one of the lithe dancers or half-naked chorines of the Folies, but a sad-eyed blonde barmaid. Anchoring the work on the reality of her poignant expression, he created around her a dazzling world of colored reflections, glistening surfaces, artfully distorted perspectives and a network of vibrant brushstrokes. Yet somehow all the parts of the picture coalesce into a brilliant whole. Comments on the painting at its first exhibition in 1882 ranged from "vulgar" to "triumphant." But the perceptive critic Ernest Chesneau had it right when he wrote that it marked "the artist's conquest of external phenomena."

Gazing wearily, distractedly, from the center of Manet's canvas is the sturdy model Suzon. Her tired and rather bored expression may be largely a result of posing for long hours in Manet's studio—he had made sketches of the bar on the spot—but it lends reality to her role as a barmaid. In a curious turn of circumstance that further linked artist and model, Suzon later became the mistress of Manet's friend and first biographer, Edmond Bazire.

178

Bar at the Folies-Bergère, 1882

Having been awarded a medal at the Salon of 1881, Manet was privileged to submit work to the 1882 Salon without having it approved by the usual jury. He sent two paintings, a portrait of a young actress and *Bar at the Folies-Bergère (left)*.

It is a puzzling picture, bold and powerful, but disturbingly contradictory. On inspection, it becomes clear that the scene behind the barmaid is reflected in a mirror. But the mirror image seems to defy normal visual perception. The barmaid is seen face on, yet her reflection is off to the right, leading to the speculation that Manet's real point of view (and the viewer's) is far to the left. Also unsettling is the fact that the top-hatted gentleman speaking to the barmaid is disproportionately large: logic dictates that since he is farther from the mirror he should appear smaller. Thus, the mirror seems to have a reality of its own. And this is evidently Manet's aim. What he has created is a reality of light and color: as the Impressionists used a lake or river as an excuse to explore light, so Manet employs this mirror. Seen in it are the reflections of real things—the bottles on the bar, some of his friends in the background audience, the truncated legs of a trapeze artist dangling from the upper left. But Manet is interested more in the pictorial autonomy of the objects than in expressing their meaning as items of everyday experience.

Nevertheless, what unifies the picture and keeps it from being a cold, abstract exploration of light and color, is Manet's clear enjoyment of this sensuous world of pleasure. The pretty girl (her corsage elegantly echoed in the vase before her), the colors, shapes and textures of the bottles, fruit and flowers (Manet has even signed his name on the bottle at the left), all these things blend into a dazzling whole. The essential quality of the painting, as critic Chesneau wrote, consists in Manet's vision of things, "of their coloration, of their luminous vibration, of their fluctuating and transient appearance, so fugitive and swift." In conquering "external phenomena," Manet stretched the range of art's techniques—and catapulted painting into the 20th Century.

179

Chronology: Artists of Manet's Era

1750   1800   1850   1900

FRANCE

JACQUES LOUIS DAVID 1748-1825

PIERRE PRUD'HON 1758-1823

JEAN-AUGUSTE DOMINIQUE INGRES 1780-1867

THÉODORE GÉRICAULT 1791-1824

CAMILLE COROT 1796-1875

EUGÈNE DELACROIX 1798-1863

CONSTANTIN GUYS 1802-1892

MARC-GABRIEL-CHARLES GLEYRE (Swiss) 1808-1874

HONORÉ DAUMIER 1808-1879

THÉODORE ROUSSEAU 1812-1867

JEAN FRANÇOIS MILLET 1814-1875

THOMAS COUTURE 1815-1879

JEAN-LOUIS-ERNEST MEISSONIER 1815-1891

CHARLES FRANÇOIS DAUBIGNY 1817-1878

GUSTAVE COURBET 1819-1877

NADAR (GASPARD FÉLIX TOURNACHON) 1820-1910

MARCELLIN-GILBERT DESBOUTIN 1823-1902

EUGÈNE BOUDIN 1824-1898

JEAN-LÉON GÉROME 1824-1904

CHARLES-JOSUAH CHAPLIN 1825-1891

ALBERT DE BALLEROY 1828-1873

CAMILLE PISSARRO 1830-1903

ÉDOUARD MANET 1832-1883

FÉLIX BRACQUEMOND 1833-1914

EDGAR DEGAS 1834-1917

ZACHARIE ASTRUC 1835-1907

JAMES TISSOT 1836-1902

HENRI FANTIN-LATOUR 1836-1904

EMILE-AUGUSTE CAROLUS-DURAN 1838-1917

PAUL CÉZANNE 1839-1906

ODILON REDON 1840-1916

CLAUDE MONET 1840-1926

FRÉDÉRIC BAZILLE 1841-1871

BERTHE MORISOT 1841-1895

PIERRE AUGUSTE RENOIR 1841-1919

GUSTAVE CAILLEBOTTE 1848-1894

PAUL GAUGUIN 1848-1903

GEORGES SEURAT 1859-1891

PAUL SIGNAC 1863-1935

HENRI MARIE RAYMOND DE TOULOUSE-LAUTREC 1864-1901

ENGLAND

JOHN CROME 1768-1821

J.M.W. TURNER 1775-1851

JOHN CONSTABLE 1776-1837

ALFRED STEVENS 1817-1875

DANTE GABRIEL ROSSETTI 1828-1882

ALPHONSE LEGROS 1837-1911

ALFRED SISLEY 1839-1899

HOLLAND

JOHAN BARTHOLD JONGKIND 1819-1891

VINCENT VAN GOGH 1853-1890

UNITED STATES

JAMES ABBOTT McNEILL WHISTLER 1834-1903

WINSLOW HOMER 1836-1910

MARY CASSATT 1845-1926

JOHN SINGER SARGENT 1856-1925

1750   1800   1850   1900

Manet's predecessors, contemporaries and successors are grouped chronologically according to country. The bands correspond to the life-spans of the artists.

Bibliography

*Paperback

MANET—HIS LIFE AND WORKS

Bataille, George, *Manet*, Translated by A. Wainhouse and J. Emmons. Skira Inc., 1955.

Courthion, Pierre and Pierre Cailler (editors), *Portrait of Manet by Himself and His Contemporaries*. Translated by Michael Ross. Cassell & Co., Ltd., London, 1960.

Hamilton, George Heard, *Manet and His Critics*. Yale University Press, 1954.

Hanson, Anne Coffin, *Édouard Manet, 1832-1883* (exhibition catalogue). Philadelphia Museum of Art, 1966.

Moreau-Nélaton, Étienne, *Manet Raconté par Lui-même*. Laurens, Paris, 1926.

Perruchot, Henri, *La Vie de Manet*. Libraire Hachette, Paris, 1959.

Proust, Antonin, *Édouard Manet: Souvenirs*. Laurens, Paris, 1913.

Richardson, John, *Manet*. Phaidon Publishers Inc., 1967.

Sandblad, Nils Gösta, *Manet: Three Studies in Artistic Conception*. CWK Gleerup, Lund, 1954.

Tabarant, A., *Manet et Ses Oeuvres*. Libraire Gallimard, Paris, 1947.

ON OTHER PAINTERS

Bazin, Germain, *French Impressionists in the Louvre*. Translated by S. Cunliffe-Owen. Harry N. Abrams, Inc., 1958.

Boggs, Jean Sutherland, *Drawings by Degas*. City Art Museum of St. Louis, 1966.

Bouret, Jean, *Degas*. Translated by D. Woodward. Tudor Publishing Company, 1965.

Cabanne, Pierre, *Edgar Degas*. Translated by M. L. Landa. Universe Books, 1958.

Cogniat, Raymond, *Monet and His World*. Thames & Hudson, London, 1966.

Daulte, François, *Sisley Landscapes*. Translated by Diana Imber. International Art Book, Lausanne, 1962.

Fosca, François, *Degas*. Translated by James Emmons. Editions d'Art Albert Skira, Geneva, 1954.

Geffroy, Gustave, *Claude Monet: Sa Vie, Son Oeuvre* (2 vols.). Les Editions G. Crès, Paris, 1924.

Larkin, Oliver W., *Daumier: Man of His Time*. McGraw-Hill, Inc., 1966.

Mack, Gerstle, *Gustave Courbet*. Alfred A. Knopf, 1951.

Rewald, John, *Camille Pissarro*. Harry N. Abrams, Inc., 1963.

Degas Sculpture: The Complete Works. Translated by John Coleman and Noel Moul-ton. Thames & Hudson, London, 1957.

Rouart, Denis, *Claude Monet*. Introduction and conclusion by Léon Degand. Translated by James Emmons. Editions d'Art Albert Skira, Geneva, 1958.

Valéry, Paul, *Degas, Manet, Morisot*. Translated by D. Paul. Pantheon Books, 1960.

ART-HISTORICAL AND CULTURAL BACKGROUND

Baudelaire, Charles, *Art in Paris 1845-1862*. Translated and edited by Jonathan Mayne. Phaidon Publishers Inc., 1965.

The Painter of Modern Life and Other Essays. Translated and edited by Jonathan Mayne. Phaidon Publishers Inc., 1964.

Braive, Michel F., *The Era of the Photograph: A Social History*. Translated by David Britt. Thames & Hudson, London, 1966.

Courthion, Pierre, *Paris in Our Time*. Translated by Stuart Gilbert. Editions d'Art Albert Skira, Geneva, 1957.

Crespelle, J. P., *Les Maîtres de la Belle Époque*. Libraire Hachette, Paris, 1966.

Laffont, Robert (general editor), *Paris and Its People: An Illustrated History*. Translated by Isabel Quigly and Barbara Bray. Methuen & Co., Ltd., London.

Leymarie, Jean, *Impressionism* (2 vols.). Translated by James Emmons. Editions d'Art Albert Skira, Geneva, 1955.

Moore, George, *Confessions of a Young Man.** Capricorn Books, 1959.

Moskowitz, Ira, *Drawings of the Masters: French Impressionists*. Shorewood Publishers, Inc., 1962.

Novotny, Fritz, *Painting and Sculpture in Europe, 1780-1880*. The Pelican History of Art Series. Penguin Books, Inc., 1960.

Newhall, Beaumont, *The History of Photography from 1839 to the Present Day*. The Museum of Modern Art with the George Eastman House, 1964.

Pollack, Peter, *The Picture History of Photography*. Harry N. Abrams, Inc., 1958.

Pool, Phoebe, *Impressionism.** Frederick A. Praeger, 1967.

Rewald, John, *The History of Impressionism*. The Museum of Modern Art, 1961.

Sloane, Joseph C., *French Painting between the Past and the Present: Artists, Critics, and Traditions, from 1848 to 1870*. Princeton University Press, 1951.

Venturi, Lionello, *Les Archives de l'Impressionnisme*. Durand-Ruel, Paris, 1939.

Picture Credits

Sources for the illustrations appear below. Credits for pictures from left to right are separated by semicolons, from top to bottom by dashes.

SLIPCASE—Lee Boltin
Front End Papers—The Fogg Art Museum
Back End Papers—John Savage, collection of Mr. David Daniels

CHAPTER 1: 6—Pierre Boulat. 9—The Solomon R. Guggenheim Museum. 10,11—Frank Lerner. 12—Eric Schaal. 14—Giraudon. 17—Archives Nationales. 18—Roger Viollet—Photo Bulloz. 21—Photo Bulloz. 23—The Art Institute of Chicago—The New York Public Library, S. P. Avery Collection. 26—Bibliothèque Nationale, Paris. 29—Derek Bayes. 30,31—National Gallery, London. 32,33—National Gallery of Art, Washington, D.C. 34,35—Giraudon—Metropolitan Museum of Art; Scala.

CHAPTER 2: 36—Eddy van der Veen. 38—New York Public Library. 41—Photo Bulloz—Collection Sirot. 45—Photo Bulloz. 46—Giraudon. 47—Réunion des Musées Nationaux. 48—Henry B. Beville. 49—Foto Blauel. 50 through 53—Eddy van der Veen. 54,55—Philadelphia Museum of Art, A. J. Wyatt; Eddy van der Veen—From the Collection of Mr. and Mrs. Paul Mellon.

CHAPTER 3: 56—Giraudon. 60—© The Frick Collection—Photo Bulloz. 62—Trustees of the British Museum. 64—Photo Bulloz. 66—Bibliothèque Nationale, Paris. 67—The Art Institute of Chicago. 69—Scala. 70,71—Eddy van der Veen. 72,73—Stadtische Kunsthalle, Mannheim; A. J. Wyatt. 74,75—Frank Lerner. 76,77—Agraci; Scala. 78—Agraci. 79—Pierre Boulat.

CHAPTER 4: 80—Eddy van der Veen. 82—Photo Bulloz. 83—The Art Institute of Chicago. 87—Charles E. Slatkin Galleries—Eddy van der Veen. 91—The New York Public Library, Astor, Lennox and Tilden Foundations. 92,93—Eddy van der Veen Courtesy Société Française de Photographie. 94—Bettmann Archive. 95—Archives Photographique except bottom right Bettmann Archive. 96,97—Eddy van der Veen Courtesy André Jammes; Archives Photographique. 98—George Eastman House—© A. Frequin, La Musée Boymans van Beuningen—courtesy Aaron Scharf, comparison discovered by Suzanne Eisendieck and first published by John Rewald; The National Gallery, London. 99—Photo Bulloz courtesy Musée du Louvre—Bibliothèque Nationale, Paris. 100,101—George Eastman House.

CHAPTER 5: 102—The New York Public Library, Astor, Lennox and Tilden Foundations. 104—Map by Rafael Palacios. 106,108—Bibliothèque Nationale, Paris. 110—Drawings from the Daniels Collection-Exhibition Catalogue, Fogg Art Museum, Harvard University, 1968—Museum of Modern Art. 113—Scala. 114,115—Eddy van der Veen; Foto Blauel—Wadsworth Atheneum, Hartford, Conn. 116—Giraudon; Metropolitan Museum of Art; Collection Mr. and Mrs. Paul Mellon—Derek Bayes; National Museum, Stockholm; Agraci—Lee Boltin; Eric Schaal; Paul Rosenberg Co.—Henry B. Beville; Giraudon. 117—Eddy van der Veen; Museum of Modern Art; Museum of Fine Arts, Boston; Yves Debraine—Museum of Fine Arts, Boston; Philadelphia Museum of Art; Metropolitan Museum of Art; Giraudon—National Museum, Stockholm; Lee Boltin; Frank Lerner; Minneapolis Institute of Art—Réunion des Musées Nationaux; Yves Debraine; Derek Bayes; Yves Debraine. 118—Giraudon—Eddy van der Veen. 119—Giraudon. 120,121—Museum of Art, Carnegie Institute, Pittsburgh, Elton Schnellbacher. 122—Sterling and Francine Clark Art Institute—Pallas Gallery, London. 123—Courtauld Institute, London. 124,125—Henry B. Beville. 126—Lee Boltin—Eddy van der Veen. 127—Giraudon—Lee Boltin. 128,129—Eddy van der Veen. 130,131—Art Institute of Chicago; Giraudon.

CHAPTER 6: 132—National Gallery of Art, Washington, D.C. 134—Roger Viollet—Bibliothèque Nationale, Paris. 136—The New York Public Library—The New York Public Library, S. P. Avery Collection. 142—Rheinisches Bildarchiv, Cologne—Cliché des Musées Nationaux. 145—Foto Kleinhempel. 146,147—Collection Mr. and Mrs. Paul Mellon—Giraudon; Derek Bayes. 148—Collection Mr. and Mrs. Paul Mellon. 149—Frank Lerner. 150—Yves Debraine—Eddy van der Veen. 151—Eddy van der Veen. 152,153—Sandak Inc.—Henry B. Beville. 154,155—The Art Institute of Chicago—Agraci; Lee Boltin. 156—Scala. 157—Pierre Boulat. 158—Collection Norton Simon, Los Angeles. 159—Philadelphia Museum of Art. 160—Henry B. Beville. 161—Pierre Boulat. 162 through 167—Leonard von Matt from Rapho Guillumette.

CHAPTER 7: 168—Sterling and Francine Clark Art Institute, Williamstown, Massachusetts. 170,171—Eddy van der Veen. 177 through 183—Derek Bayes. 187—Metropolitan Museum of Art.

Acknowledgments

For his help in the production of this book the author and editors particularly wish to thank Maurice Sérullaz, Conservateur du Cabinet des Dessins au Musée du Louvre. They also wish to thank the following people: Jean Adhémar, Conservateur du Cabinet des Estampes, Bibliothèque Nationale, Paris; Roseline Bacou, Conservateur du Cabinet des Dessins, Musée du Louvre; Catherine Belenger, Service des Relations Extérieures du Musée du Louvre; Adeline Cacan, Conservateur du Petit Palais, Paris; Courtauld Galleries, London; François Daulte, Lausanne; F. Fenyö, Szépmüveszeti Muzeum, Budapest; David Finch, French Institute, New York; Madame Guynet-Pechadre, Conservateur, Service Photographique, Musée du Louvre; André Jammes, Paris; Cécile de Jandin, Bibliothécaire, Cabinet des Estampes, Bibliothèque Nationale, Paris; Samuel Josefowitz, Lausanne; Jacqueline Le Clerc, Service des Relations Extérieures, Musée du Louvre; Alex Maguy, Paris; Marie Montembault, Cabinet des Dessins, Musée du Louvre; The National Museum, Stockholm; Leopold Reidemeister, Bruecke Museum, Berlin; Denis Rouart, Conservateur de Musée des Beaux Arts de Nancy; Aaron Scharf, London; Otfried Schroeder, Kunsthalle, Hamburg; Franca Sironi, Editioni Rizzoli, Milano; Joseph C. Sloane, Chairman of the Department of Art, University of North Carolina, Chapel Hill; Lucien Solanet, Paris; Germaine Tureau, Chief, Section Commeréiale de la Photothèque des Musées Nationaux, Paris; Daniel Wildenstein, Paris and New York.

THE METROPOLITAN MUSEUM OF ART, BEQUEST OF MRS. H. O. HAVEMEYER, 1929.

George Moore, 1879. A detail of Manet's pastel portrait appears in color on the slipcase.

Key to paintings reproduced on pages 116-117

MONET

1866-1867	1869	1875-1878	1877	1884	1905	c. 1920
WOMEN IN THE GARDEN Jeu de Paume, Musée du Louvre, Paris	LA GRENOUILLÉRE The Metropolitan Museum of Art, New York Bequest of Mrs H. O. Havemeyer, 1929	WOMAN WITH PARASOL - MADAME MONET AND HER SON Collection of Mr. and Mrs. Paul Mellon	SAINT-LAZARE STATION Musée Marmottan, Paris	HAYSTACKS Collection of Mr. and Mrs. Josef Rosensaft, New York	ROUEN CATHEDRAL, SUNSET Museum of Fine Arts, Boston, Juliana Cheney Edwards Collection	WATER-GARDEN AT GIVERNY Musée des Beaux-Arts, Grenoble

RENOIR

1867	1869	c. 1875	1883	1884-1887	1890	c. 1910-1917
LISE Folkwang Museum, Essen	LA GRENOUILLÉRE National Museum, Stockholm	ROAD CLIMBING THROUGH LONG GRASS Jeu de Paume, Musée de Louvre, Paris	DANCE AT BOUGIVAL Museum of Fine Arts, Boston	THE BATHERS Philadelphia Museum of Art, Carroll S. Tyson Collection	IN THE MEADOW The Metropolitan Museum of Art, New York, Bequest of Samuel A. Lewisohn, 1951	ODALISQUE WITH TURKISH SLIPPERS Jeu de Paume, Musée du Louvre, Paris

PISSARRO

c. 1864	1870	1872	1874	1878	1888	1898
THE ROAD Collection of Dr. and Mrs. Gordon Pollock, New York	LOUVECIENNES, THE ROAD TO VERSAILLES E. G. Bührle Foundation, Zurich	SNOW AT LOUVECIENNES Private Collection	PEASANT WOMEN WITH A WHEELBARROW National Museum, Stockholm	PARK IN PONTOISE Collection of Mr. & Mrs. Benjamin M. Reeves, New York	APPLE HARVEST AT ERAGNY Dallas Museum of Fine Arts	AVENUE DE L'OPÉRA, PARIS IN THE RAIN The Minneapolis Institute of Art

SISLEY

1866	1874	1878	1888	1892	1893
STREET IN MARLOTTE Albright-Knox Art Gallery, Buffalo	THE REGATTA AT MOULSEY Jeu de Paume, Musée du Louvre, Paris	SNOW AT LOUVECIENNES Jeu de Paume, Musée du Louvre, Paris	THE BRIDGE AND MILLS AT MORET IN SUMMER Collection of G.C. Salmanowitz, Geneva	STREET IN MORET-SUR-LOING Fitzwilliam Museum, Cambridge England	CHURCH AT MORET Private Collection, Lausanne

Index

Numerals in italics indicate a picture of the subject mentioned. Unless otherwise specified, all listed art works are by Manet. Dimensions are given in inches; height precedes width.

189

The text for this book was photocomposed in Bodoni Book, a typeface named for its Italian designer, Giambattista Bodoni (1740-1813). One of the earliest modern typefaces, Bodoni Book differs from more evenly weighted old-style characters in the greater contrast between thick and thin parts of letters. The Bodoni character is vertical with a thin, straight serif.

✕

PRODUCTION STAFF FOR TIME INCORPORATED

*John L. Hallenbeck (Vice President and Director of Production),
Robert E. Foy and Caroline Ferri
Text photocomposed under the direction of Albert J. Dunn and Arthur J. Dunn*